How to Publish a

Bestselling

Book

. . . and Sell it WORLDWIDE
Based on Value, Not Price!

How to Publish a *Bestselling Book*

... and Sell it WORLDWIDE Based on Value, Not Price!

Kim Staflund

How to Publish a Bestselling Book
. . . and Sell It WORLDWIDE Based on Value, Not Price!

eBook ISBN: 978-0-9864869-9-9
Paperback ISBN: 978-0-9864869-8-2

With special thanks to the following valued contributors to this book:

Kathleen O'Connor, Copy editing and fact checking
Ted Ruybal, Graphic design of cover and interior
John Rempel, Graphic design of interior graphics
Susan Chambers, Proofreading
Tia Leschke, Indexing
Melissa Leech and Kim Staflund, Additional proofreading

Added thanks to all who helped with the author photo:

Gregory Morton of Life Photo Studios, Photography
Shae Barry of DICIB? Does it come in black?, Make-up artistry
Heather Marshall of Lavish Salon, Hairstyling
Happy Choice Nail & Spa, Northland Mall, Manicure

Additional copies of this book may be ordered by visiting the PPG Online Bookstore at:

shop.polishedpublishinggroup.com

Due to the dynamic nature of the Internet, any website addresses mentioned within this book might have been changed or discontinued since its publication. While reading this book will not guarantee that you will become a bestselling author, doing the recommended practices will definitely improve your chances of becoming a bestselling author.

"Quality isn't something that can be argued into an article or promised into it. It must be put there. If it isn't put there, the finest sales talk in the world won't act as a substitute."

~Joseph Campbell

For entrepreneurs the world over

Table of Contents

PREFACE

In 2013, I launched *How to Publish a Book in Canada . . . and Sell Enough Copies to Make a Profit!* to address the frequently asked questions that are specific to Canadian individuals and businesses that wish to publish their work. This book was (and continues to be) a tremendous learning tool for many—so much so that it became a bestseller on Amazon within its first month and a half and has spawned even more questions from aspiring authors all across North America and even "across the pond" in the United Kingdom and other parts of Europe. You've asked and the Polished Publishing Group (PPG) has listened. Introducing *How to Publish a Bestselling Book . . . and Sell It WORLDWIDE Based on Value, Not Price!* which has been written for all the aspiring authors and business professionals who wish to produce a book that presents them as professional writers and industry experts in their fields.

Whether you're writing a fictional novel, a cookbook, or a "how to" book, publishing a book is a business venture. All authors are entrepreneurs. And the first thing every entrepreneur should ask himself or herself is this: do I offer the best *value* in my field, or do I offer the best *price*? This is a vitally important question to ask of yourself <u>before</u> you begin the publishing process of your book. Why? Because, if you offer the best value in your field, you need to promote your business (and everything related to it—*including* your book!) using value-based selling. If you offer the best price, you need to promote your book using price-based selling. Consistency is the key to long-term success no matter what industry you're in.

I've read quite a few ebooks, written by self-published, "independent" authors (a.k.a. "indie" authors) and sold for less than $5 per copy online, that offer all kinds of advice and impressive statistics regarding how to publish and sell a bestselling book. Then I've scrolled to the back of these books to try to find the source(s) for these alleged statistics—but I could find no bibliography or supporting back matter of any kind. This appeared more than a little suspicious to someone with over twenty years of experience in the field of book publishing. Rule One in producing a *professional*-quality, non-fiction book of any kind is this: If you're going to add any statistics to your content whatsoever, you've got to be able to show your readers the legitimate sources where they can verify the authenticity of these claims. Your book needs to contain *all* the necessary interior components—a properly formatted front matter, body, and back matter—along with a professionally designed book cover that contains compelling back cover marketing copy. Otherwise, it will appear to be nothing more than false advertising that reeks of amateurism—and that's suicide for any professional.

If you want to produce a book that presents you as an industry expert in your field, it must be completed by an industry expert in the book publishing field. That's exactly what PPG is. There's a right way to do this if you want to create a professional-quality bestselling book, while still maintaining 100% copyright ownership of both your words and your artwork. In this book, we'll discuss the whole book publishing process in fair detail to help you understand what needs to be prepared in advance of submitting your book to PPG for publication.

We'll discuss those little extras that one must do if one wishes to stand out from the rest (e.g., including an index in the back of a non-fiction book). PPG puts all its authors' books through the proper, complete publishing process—one that you simply won't be able to achieve by yourself—while allowing you to maintain full copyright ownership of the entire end product.

By the time you're done reading this book, hopefully you'll have gained some valuable insight into what it *truly* takes to produce a saleable book and how to market it to your desired demographic. Better yet, you'll have all the tools you need to get that book into the hands of those desired customers all around the world, land on a coveted bestseller list in your area, and earn a healthy profit in the process. That is my wish for you.

Sincerely,

Kim Staflund

Founder and publisher of Polished Publishing Group (PPG)

FOREWORD

Hindsight: what a wonderful word, one that implies understanding of events after they've happened. If we all had the gift of hindsight, life would be so much simpler and many of our questions would become unnecessary. I am very fortunate to have hindsight at my fingertips when it comes to the self-publishing versus trade publishing conundrum because I own a copy of *How to Publish a Book in Canada . . . and Sell Enough Copies to Make a Profit!*. I was proud to join Kim Staflund at one of her book signings and to purchase a copy for her to sign for me because I know what it's like to have a signing and feel the joy that comes along with someone excitedly handing you a copy of your blood, sweat, and tears, which you hope will inspire him or her and enhance his or her life in some way.

Many, many years ago, I sat at a computer screen and watched as a novel unfolded before my very eyes. I cried and laughed and watched in amazement, as my fingers swept lightly across the keys, creating a story that I didn't even know existed within me. I passed around the manuscript to friends, co-workers and family who were kind enough to be honest in their evaluation of my "book." Their feedback was positive and created enough inspiration for me to begin the process of sending off the manuscript to trade publishers within North America. Ugh. After numerous attempts to have my manuscript published and all the work done for me (in my mind), I took my positive but "not at this time" responses and shelved them—for years!

During this extensive hiatus, I met Kim. With our boys in the same school class, we saw each other periodically and shared our book interests. I read her books and she read mine. I watched as she self-published and painstakingly worked on sales and marketing, not fully understanding the frustrations she was going through until the day she announced her new creation: Polished Publishing Group (PPG), a supportive self-publishing company that allowed 100% of the finished product to belong to the author. Here was a culmination of her efforts and struggles in the industry to prevent others from going through the same experience regarding publishing; now that was worth considering! I took my weathered manuscript down from the shelf, dusted it off, took a deep breath, and called Kim.

The process of publishing with PPG in all areas was extremely enjoyable and a major learning experience. My concerns and questions were met and answered until the result of all the hard work was revealed in a beautiful, professional paperback copy of my book with my photo on the back: a dream made into reality! However, (and this is where the hindsight comes back into play) for as much as I had Kim and her staff at my fingertips, how I wish that her own book, *How to Publish a Book in Canada*, had been available to me before I had begun the process. All you lucky people out there who have it now, and will also be holding this enhancement of her knowledge of the publishing industry, *How to Publish a Bestselling Book . . . and Sell it WORLDWIDE Based on Value not Price!*, will be able to go into publishing your own books with a keen understanding of the publishing industry and the process itself. Now, people outside of Canada can benefit from Kim's knowledge and learn how to prepare a manuscript and sell the books when published. You won't have as many questions as I did because you will have the answers beforehand and can proceed joyfully, knowing that you will finally reach your dream of publishing your own work.

When I first wrote my manuscript, self-publishing was perceived as the "other option," the one where you weren't of sufficient interest for a trade publisher to pick you up and shoot your book to the top of the charts. Well, now, life has moved on hasn't it? We are now surrounded by e-this and e-that, along with social media; thus, the rules have changed drastically. With the balance between physical books—offering their scent of the unknown and dog-eared knowledge—and the convenience and intrigue of the ebook with virtual paper edges and electronic sticky notes, the possibilities are endless and Kim outlines all these options in her books.

I urge all of you would-be authors to take the plunge and go ahead with your dreams after gaining the knowledge from Kim's books. I was terrified to my very core with this whole process and still am when it comes to sales and marketing; however, with guidance, I can make the effort, and knowledge is still powerful, so I absorb and take the plunge anyway. The essence of my own book, *Soul Searching*, comes into play here. Within its pages, it weaves an understanding of life that reflects our own lives as we live them day by day, allowing us, perhaps, to make more beneficial choices and to understand all the opportunities that we face in life and death: the two most intriguing experiences that we know. If I had read my own book when I was twenty, it would have saved me a lot of time—just as I know having Kim's book will save many others ahead of me. I knew that Kim's presence in my life was significant when timing and knowledge blended to allow me an opportunity to offer my story to others, just as she has been able to offer you hers. Maybe this is your time; the fact that you have this book in your hands tells you that at least you have the opportunity before you.

As I end my brief words here and you start upon yours, and as an author of a fiction novel, I want you to know that the information in Kim's books can be applied to fiction and to non-fiction. Your published book has become your own business and you will need information and techniques to make it successful. Kim has provided these techniques, and her book has become a bestseller; therefore, you or I too can become successful and can publish a bestselling book. Believe me when I say that you might never be satisfied with your constant overlooking of commas and parenthesis and sentence structure, etc., but you will be satisfied when an excited someone passes you a copy of your shiny and polished book and says, "Would you please sign this for me . . . ?"

A.R. Jones, Author of *Soul Searching*
Adobe eBook ISBN: 978-0-9880381-1-0
Paperback ISBN: 978-0-9880381-0-3
Copyright 2012 A.R. Jones, All Rights Reserved
(Available for sale at ARJones.ca, on Kobo, Amazon's group of sites, and all other distribution networks and retailers mentioned in this book. That said, the best place to get an *author-signed* copy is directly from the author's website listed here.)

SECTION ONE:

The Types of
Book Publishers

"By the work one knows the workmen."

~Jean De La Fontaine

WHERE TO BEGIN?

As a business owner, doing one's due diligence is especially important when it comes to finding a suitable partner to help you publish a book. In this day and age, so much information is out there on this topic that it can be quite overwhelming and more than a little bit confusing. What road should you take? Which choice will bring you the best return on investment? Who can best help you to achieve your goals?

Well that all depends. What are your goals? The very first thing that *everyone* should do—individuals and businesses alike—is to sit down with a pen and paper and make a list of the reasons *why* they wish to publish their books and what exactly they wish to gain from doing it. This is the first step in determining which avenue to take toward fulfilling your goals.

TEN QUESTIONS TO ASK YOURSELF BEFORE PUBLISHING YOUR BOOK

1. Who am I? Do I offer the best *value* or the best *price* in my field?

2. Who is my target audience? What demographic group am I after (i.e., what gender, what age, et cetera)?

3. What is my deadline for this project? Do I need this book completed quickly (within around six weeks, give or take), fairly soon (within three to six months), or can I afford to wait up to two years for the final product to be printed?

4. Am I willing to invest my own time and money into this project or do I want it published free of charge?

5. Do I want to earn a profit from this book?

6. Do I want to produce this book as a paperback, hardcover, or ebook—or all three formats?

7. Do I want to have complete creative control over the design of my book, do I want to collaborate with a professional over the design of my book, or am I willing to give up majority creative control to the publisher?

8. Would I prefer to work with a knowledgeable project manager who can guide me through the book publishing process from start to finish, including arranging all the contracts and dealing with the various vendors (editors, designers, et cetera) on my behalf, or am I fine with (and have the time for) doing the bulk of this work myself?

9. Do I want to keep 100 percent of the copyright ownership of my story (words)?

10. Do I want to keep 100 percent of the copyright ownership of my book cover (artwork)?

After deciding which of these points is most important, the next step is to prioritize your choices. For example, the authors who value both a quick turnaround and profit should now decide which of those is most important and put it at the top. From there, you should move down the list and compare the remaining questions until you have created a personal hierarchy of values. Then it will be time to look at the various book publishing business models to determine which model best matches your personal list of needs.

THE TYPES OF BOOK PUBLISHERS

Authors have three primary book publishing business models to choose from, regardless of whether they wish to produce an electronic book (ebook), paperback, or hardcover: (a) traditional (trade) publishing; (b) vanity publishing (which is basically book production and formatting for self-publishing "indie" authors); and (c) supported self-publishing (also sometimes referred to as assisted self-publishing or hybrid publishing). Each of these business models has its pros and its cons. To determine which business model is best for you (for your particular book project, for your personal hierarchy of values), it is important to understand the characteristics that differentiate trade publishers from vanity publishers from supportive self-publishing companies.

TRADITIONAL (TRADE) PUBLISHING

Many writers continue to envision the traditional process when they consider having a book published: seeking out a trade publisher (whether personally or via a hired agent) that will consider their type of work; mailing a query letter and sample chapter or poem to that publisher; and then anxiously awaiting a response, within three to six months, to be told whether the publisher will take on the project. More often than not, the unknown author's work is declined, and he or she must move onto the next submission with the next trade publisher, hoping that the book will eventually be accepted. Sound familiar?

Those authors who are new to the book publishing industry often view this as a personal rejection of their work. Many authors give up hope of ever being published at all. The truth is that writing quality is far from being the only determinant that trade publishers use when deciding whether to accept a manuscript for publication. Most receive hundreds (even thousands) of manuscript submissions every year from which they might select as few as one dozen new authors to work with—a discriminatingly low acceptance rate. Obviously, budget and manpower play a huge role in their decisions (as it certainly did at the literary press where I worked several years ago). But more is at play here than that, depending on the type of trade publisher you're dealing with.

Trade book publishers are typically academic scholars who are looking for books with a strong literary merit. They want the scholastic novels and poetry; so, you might have written a cookbook or industry "how to" book, for example, that falls outside their realm of academia. You might want to celebrate a professional milestone by publishing a business history book. You might have penned a cathartic account of a traumatic event that you wish to share with others to help them through something similar . . . or you might have written in any number of different genres that fall outside the traditional publisher's area of expertise. The chances are that these types of books simply won't fit with a traditional publisher's program, nor will they fit with the requirements set out by their various stakeholders. Therefore, you'll be rejected—despite your acceptable writing abilities and saleable idea. This is why it's so important to research a publishing company, ahead of time, to gain a clear understanding of the type of projects they will (and will *not*) accept.

One of the biggest myths about trade publishers is that all of them are out there actively selling *all* of their authors' books for them on a regular basis. Nothing could be further from the truth. Trade publishers focus primarily on their *front list* titles; and, once those books fall to the *back list*, the responsibility of continued promotion falls to the author.

So, what is a front list title? What is a back list title? The trade publisher I worked for years ago followed the typical schedule of many Canadian publishers in that we published two sets of books per year—one in the spring and one in the fall. Each new batch of books was considered the new front list titles, and our focus was always and only on highlighting those new books—never the old back list titles. We simply didn't have the budget, manpower, or time to focus on anything more. To clarify, once a new set of books came out, the current front list became part of the back list. So, the shelf life of any new book was from six months to a year. That's it. That was the amount of time we truly focused on any one book before moving onto the latest and greatest.

Another issue with the trade publishing sector is the fact that most (if not *all* of these publishers) follow an archaic book return policy that can detrimentally affect profits for both themselves and their authors. When a publisher marks its books as "returnable" for wholesalers and retailers, it is giving them the right to return those books, at any given time, for a full refund if they're unable to sell them—regardless of whether those books are stickered with price tags or a bit scuffed from being handled by various people.

This has always bothered me. It *still* seems wrong to me, and it *still* happens in this day and age. Think about this for a minute. Really think about it.

Now, I'm sure that there were valid reasons for doing things this way at one point, a long time ago. Maybe this bookstore return policy was some sort of incentive that publishers created to entice bookstores to buy more of their books. Maybe it was a way to help struggling booksellers stay afloat. Yet, how many manufacturers do you know of—in *any* industry—that would be able to stay in business for any length of time if their retailers were returning their products to them damaged and unsaleable for a full refund? If this happened on a regular basis, they'd be out of business very quickly. Wouldn't they? Yet it happens every day in the book publishing industry, and some people just accept it as the norm without any question whatsoever.

Authors whose work is accepted and published by trade book publishers obviously enjoy the lowest personal risk in terms of financial investment: $0. In fact, many people (myself included) often start out submitting their books to these publishers simply because it's free of charge and appears, at first glance, to be the best road toward success as an author. In this business model, the publisher assumes all the financial responsibility and risk. Sounds like a great deal for the author, doesn't it? Yes and no. Here's the trade-off. Trade publishers don't pick up the bill simply out of the kindness of their hearts. When they agree to pay for the publication of a manuscript, what they are purchasing is the *copyright* ownership of that work (whether permanently or temporarily, it varies per contract). In other words, the author must now relinquish much of his or her creative control to the publisher. The publisher has the final say on editing and design. The publisher has the final say on how the book is to be produced and marketed—because it is the publisher who now owns the book. Look at the copyright page of any book you pick up in the bookstore. Is the publisher's name listed there or the author's name? Whoever's name is listed on that page next to the © is the primary copyright owner of that book.

In terms of profits, trade authors retain only basic "publishing rights" that recognize them as the creator of the written words, and they are paid only a small royalty for any sales that the publisher makes—often as low as 10 percent of the retail price of the book. (This percentage will vary with each contract. Also sometimes, in the larger markets, authors are paid an advance before publication.) As the owner of the book, the publisher keeps all of the remaining profits. To put this into perspective, let's say a book is priced at $15 per copy retail. Ten percent of that is only $1.50. Even if the publisher is able to sell 10,000 copies of the book in one year, the author will only earn $15,000 in royalties that year. It makes much more sense for authors to approach this with an entrepreneurial mindset: buy copies of their books back from that publisher at a wholesale price of $7.50 each and then try to sell all of them directly themselves. Although they won't earn royalties on these wholesale author copies, they will still stand to earn more per unit if they sell them at full price without a middleman between them and their buyer. Make sense? (Even with a middleman, like a bookstore or retail outlet, the author still stands to earn more per unit by selling his or her own wholesale copies.)

In addition to the loss of copyright ownership, another potential disadvantage to this type of book publishing is the timeline. It can take from three months to a year for authors to learn whether their manuscripts have been accepted for publication; and, if accepted, it can take another full year for their books to be published—sometimes more. It takes a long time to cultivate the gold standard in literary book publishing. Trade publishers put each and every manuscript through a very thorough and professional process of substantive and stylistic editing, copy editing, graphic design, indexing (in the case of non-fiction books), and proofreading to ensure a polished and saleable result. Several eyes are on every raw manuscript and galley proof all the way through the process to ensure that 99 percent of every last error is caught and corrected before it goes to print.

For those who regard a limited upfront financial risk above all else in their personal hierarchy of values, and whose manuscripts fit well with a traditional publisher's program, the trade book publishing route might be the right one to take. Definitely, it is something special to receive a letter of acceptance in the mail from a respected scholarly person that says, "You are one of very few people chosen for our publishing line-up this year. We want to work with *you*."

For those authors who have different priorities—a quick turn-around, personal satisfaction, profit, maintained copyright ownership and creative control, and professional saleability—other book publishing business models should be considered. Other choices are available.

VANITY PUBLISHING (BOOK PRODUCTION AND FORMATTING FOR SELF-PUBLISHING "INDIE" AUTHORS)

The vanity book publishing model was introduced as an alternative for writers who were tired of waiting around to be accepted by a traditional book publisher and who had instead decided to self-publish their books themselves. As noble as the vanity publishers' intentions might be (to provide another viable alternative to aspiring authors), they are the least respected book publishing alternative of them all within publishing circles (i.e., traditional publishers, reviewers, booksellers, and distributors)—for good reason. These companies are more aptly described as book *printers* than publishers, and they've earned their notoriety by accepting and printing 100 percent of the manuscripts that are submitted to them without much consideration of quality or content—the opposite extreme of trade publishing. A vanity publisher will take what it receives and print it as is—no matter what it looks like. Not only does this reflect poorly on the vanity publisher as a service provider, but it also reflects poorly on the writer. Books that are haphazardly produced in this manner simply cannot compete in the marketplace against a professional trade publisher's finished product. There is a noticeable difference between the two.

Some of these companies run a "self-service" type of operation that allows self-publishing authors to upload their book files online (or via email) and then draft them into ebooks or into various other formats themselves, using a selection of generic template builders. Other vanity publishers are actual print shops with in-house design staff who will take your raw materials (manuscript, graphics, et cetera) and do all that formatting and typesetting for you—a slightly more professional approach. However, at the end of the day, they all share one commonality: although their staff might be fairly knowledgeable about printing and electronic file formatting, they are wholly unseasoned when it comes to the essential *publishing* practices (such as professional editing, graphic design, and proofreading) that ensure the polished end result that every serious author is after. Vanity publishers never actively encourage their clients to improve the quality of their work in any way, and this lack of improvement is truly a disservice to the serious-minded authors who wish to present themselves to the public as professionals and experts within their fields.

In the Preface section of my last book *How to Publish a Book in Canada . . . and Sell Enough Copies to Make a Profit!*, I discuss my personal experiences as an author who was trying to publish a quality book within the vanity book publishing sector. The three vanity publishers that I worked with employed *none* of the standard practices of a traditional trade book publisher— mandatory professional editing, graphic design, and proofreading—nor did they promote my books for me in any way, shape, or form. It was essentially book printing (aside from the copy editing that I insisted upon and paid for by my own choice, outside of their processes); and, although it felt good to see my work in print, in the end, the whole process lacked professionalism and the result was noticeably amateur when compared, side by side, with a trade published book. It seemed as though very little personal care and attention was given to each proofing round; rather, it felt as though my book had been rushed along a robotic assembly line during each round. Possibly one of the most frustrating parts for someone coming from a traditional publishing background was the inconsistency in the editorial style used on each of my first three books.

Most vanity publishers advertise that the authors who work with them will retain 100 percent copyright ownership of their books; however, they neglect to mention that the print-ready files for those books will be kept "under lock and key," inaccessible to those authors. In other words, they retain the copyright ownership of the artwork they created for the author (e.g., the book cover). This means those authors must always go through them to have all of their marketing materials and books printed; and, because most of these publishers use only print-on-demand (POD) printing technology, those authors stand to lose money on the larger print runs that really should be completed on either a digital or an offset press, both of which are designed specifically for larger print runs. (These types of printing options are described in more detail later on in this book.)

It costs money to print a book. That's why many vanity publishers want to keep your files to ensure that you will always print through them—because that's how they make their profit. They are printers first, after all. So that's really all you're paying for when you pre-pay the publishing package you found online that sounded something like this: "Publish your book in 30 days for as little as $799!" That price excludes professional editing, graphic design, indexing (in the case of non-fiction books), and proofreading which is why it's so cheap and can be completed so quickly. That price is the "bare bones" minimum that they can charge to entice you to print your book with them while still taking home a profit for themselves. Everything else is up to you when you choose this unsupported self-publishing route to produce your book.

Most vanity publishers will offer different sizes of publishing packages with additional add-on services that will cost a little more for those who are interested: editorial evaluations, social media marketing tips, inclusion of your book title on their next media release, et cetera. Yet, what good is any of this unless you're working with people who are properly trained to provide you with a *professional* editorial evaluation, can actually teach you *professional* sales techniques using social media, and can put a *saleable* product into your hands at the end of it all? I'll come right out and say it: it's worth very little to you, if anything at all. The vanity publisher is the only one that truly benefits from these additional revenue streams. Don't you think, from the author's standpoint, that this practice rather defeats the purpose of publishing?

One upside to the vanity-publishing model is its timeline. Manuscripts are accepted immediately upon receipt of payment and can be printed in as little as one or two months' time. Another advantage is that these printers pay a significantly higher royalty rate than trade publishers do on any copies of the book that they're able to sell on behalf of the author. Of course, as in the traditional book publishing model, authors can also purchase copies of their books at wholesale prices and sell them on their own for the best profit margin of all. One final, notable benefit to this book publishing model is that authors maintain the primary copyright ownership of their books (their words, at least); therefore, they reserve the right to sell off additional rights for additional profit down the road. This is where the *real* money is—in the sale of rights. (Copyright and the sale of rights will be described in more detail later in this book.)

The majority of vanity publishers that I've come across during my career follow the same bookstore return policy as the traditional publishers do from the unfounded fear that bookstores won't buy non-returnable books. (That's yet another myth. Yes, they *will* buy what is saleable, what their customers specifically request from them—if only one book at a time.) Yet, some other publishers have come to see it differently and they will allow their authors to make that choice for themselves.

Unlike trade publishers who divide their books into front list and back list selections with each new publishing round, and who tend only to produce their new books at specific times during the year, vanity published books can be produced at any time of the year. It's always and only a front list book, and the timeline of launch is up to the author.

For those authors who publish their books solely for personal gratification and need them completed fairly quickly, the vanity book publishing route is probably the best one to take. This route is a great option for family history books, special scrapbooks intended as gifts for loved ones, and other *non*-commercial projects.

For those with different priorities—profit, maintained copyright ownership and creative control, professional saleability—you should consider another book publishing business model. You have another choice.

SUPPORTED SELF-PUBLISHING (A.K.A. ASSISTED SELF-PUBLISHING, HYBRID PUBLISHING)

Supported self-publishing incorporates the flexibility and copyright retention of vanity publishing with the professional quality of trade publishing to provide authors with a much more balanced approach to book publishing. Balance is better because it arms authors with all the tools that they will need to sell enough copies of their books to earn a profit, and it gives them more control over whether their books become bestsellers or not.

Think of a supportive self-publishing house as a skilled project manager for self-publishing authors. Writers are considered both the author and the publisher of their books because they are recognized as the creator of the written words, plus they pay for the production of the book while retaining 100 percent copyright ownership of both their words *and* their completed artwork. The supportive self-publishing house merely assists them in producing a polished product by supplying all the tools that they will need (contracts with professional editors, designers, proofreaders, and indexers, et cetera) and facilitating the entire process from start to finish.

Professional copy editing, graphic design, and proofreading is mandatory in this book publishing business model just as it is in the traditional model. A qualified supportive self-publishing house, such as Polished Publishing Group (PPG), will employ only high calibre talent (referred to as professional work-made-for-hire vendors in each of the contracts) who have at least five years of experience in their fields—preferably more—and who are pre-screened and approved by the publishing company rather than its authors. When it comes to non-fiction books, professional indexing is also mandatory, and it is highly recommended that authors employ additional fact-checking services to ensure the accuracy of their statements.

Supportive self-publishing houses use modern printing techniques such as POD and modern marketing and distribution services (online presence) in much the same way as today's vanity publishers use them. However, an added bonus is that all finished files are returned to the authors once the publication is complete, in case they wish to print larger quantities of their books on a digital or offset press and sell them in traditional markets. The company will recommend printers to its authors and will help them to write the first one or two quote requests to put them on the right track for future reference.

When writers pay for professional support in publishing their books, they gladly maintain a strong degree of creative control throughout the publishing process. The author–self-publisher has the final say on everything from editing and design to production, and to marketing the final product. This control, combined with all the other services, ensures a quality result that will be able to compete in the marketplace—which can make a world of difference when it comes to selling books and earning any kind of profit down the road.

As a supportive self-publishing house with its authors' best interests in mind, PPG marks all of the books it sells for them as non-returnable. The authors who wish to print copies of their books and offer them to the bookstores as returnable, can do so; however, it is worth noting that, for new (unknown) authors in particular, a one-day consignment book signing event is often a better decision. (Book signings will be described in more detail in the Sales and Marketing section of this book.)

Unlike trade publishers who divide their books into front list and back list selections with each new publishing round in the spring and fall, the supportive self-publishing business model allows authors to produce books at any time of the year much like the vanity publishers produce them. The biggest benefit here is obvious: as long as you're still actively selling your book, it's still a front list title for you, isn't it? Front list books sell. It's all in the marketing, all in the presentation.

A supportive self-publishing house will accept and publish the majority of manuscripts handed to it upon receipt of 100 percent prepayment for the project, but some books will automatically be declined. If it is an obviously non-commercial project (such as a family history book or personal scrapbook) or it is obviously riddled with all kinds of typos and errors, it will be declined.

No company can be everything to everyone, and this is not the publishing business model for those types of projects. Supported self-publishing is intended for serious-minded authors with an entrepreneurial mindset who wish to earn a profit from the commercial sale of their books, and who would rather hire a professional project manager with industry expertise to help them produce that book than to spend copious hours awkwardly managing the project themselves.

Why 100 percent prepayment? There are three very good reasons.

1. The publisher must secure each professional vendor (entrepreneurs in their own rights) for each project with a 50 percent deposit before any of the work can even begin.

2. The additional money is held to ensure that funds are always available for the little issues that might come up regarding shipping and administration, and so that vendors can be paid in full immediately upon completing their portions of the project.

3. Possibly, most importantly of all, this payment is an author's commitment to himself or herself. Many authors have already procrastinated on publishing their books for several months or years as it is. It's amazing how 100 percent prepayment of a book publishing package will suddenly motivate them to get it done, once and for all, rather than completing one section only to procrastinate some more.

The publisher of PPG understands the nature of authors—because she was an author first, before she ever became a publisher. As such, every last detail of PPG's publishing process was perfected with the nature of authors in mind.

It will cost authors more than "as little as $799!" to publish a book via the supported self-publishing business model because they will be paying for more than simply printing. It will also take more than "only 30 days!" to put their books through the proper, full publishing process that will polish it to 99 percent perfection for them. On the plus side, it will take far less time than it takes through a traditional publisher (expect a minimum of three and a half months to complete one project from the time that all of the proper files, the contract, and the prepayment have been received). You might also be pleasantly surprised by just how affordable it really is when you browse the PPG online store (Polished Publishing Group, 2013b).

Another upside is that supportive self-publishing houses pay a significantly higher royalty rate than trade publishers pay on any copies of the book they're able to sell on behalf of the author—up to 40 percent of all profits earned on the sale of the book (Polished Publishing Group, 2013c). Also, as with every other publishing model, authors can purchase copies of their books straight from their publisher at wholesale prices to sell on their own.

You will have five additional advantages to using the supportive self-publishing business model employed by PPG:

1. **Modern, Eco-friendly, affordable book publishing methods:**

    PPG operates in a paperless, virtual office environment. The company's publishing processes are completely electronic, which boosts productivity and makes information sharing much easier and much more affordable from any location with Internet access anywhere in the world.

    When I first started PPG out of my home, I had visions of moving myself and my staff into a nice office space within one or two years, once I'd grown the company large enough to afford it. As time went on, I realized that this move was completely unnecessary. In this day and age, with the help of online tools such as Skype, YouSendIt, DropBox, PayPal, and various other cloud computing solutions, it is entirely possible to run a professional book publishing company in a virtual office environment. Everything that can be accomplished in the traditional office environment can also be accomplished in a virtual office environment—and, even better, at a fraction of the cost! The company saves thousands of dollars in office leasing costs alone, which allows us to pass those savings onto our authors while still paying our professional vendors a fair price for their services. This means we can hire the best talent possible while still keeping our costs down. Therefore, PPG continues to operate in a virtual office environment to this day—and we probably always will.

2. **Author-tailoured ISBNs:**

PPG will put the author–self-publisher's primary contact information on each book's international standard book number (ISBN) application form to ensure that the ISBN is linked to the true copyright owner of the book—the author–self-publisher.

For our Canadian authors, we'll obtain your Canadian ISBN for you (because we live in the same territory); however, we can also gladly work with authors outside of Canada who provide us with ISBNs for each edition of their books (e.g., one for the ebook version, another separate ISBN for the hardcover version, and another separate ISBN for the paperback version) from their own countries. (The reason behind assigning country-specific ISBNs will be discussed in the copyright section of this book.)

3. **Convenient payment options:**

All purchases made through the PPG Online Store can be completed using PayPal, eTransfer (in Canada), cheque, or money order.

Online ordering is made easy with PayPal. Not only does it provide a safe and secure transfer of funds from a buyer's credit card or bank account directly to PPG, but it also converts the currency exchange to Canadian funds for you. (It is worth noting that having PPG's prices listed in CDN exchange rate is especially enticing for our American authors and others abroad whose currency is worth a bit more.)

4. **Author-tailoured printing options:**

    When authors choose PPG to support them in self-publishing, not only will they retain the copyright ownership of their books, but PPG will also give the final print-ready files to the rightful owner—the author–self-publisher.

    This means that, at any time that authors decide to print larger runs (100+ physical copies) of their books to warehouse and distribute on their own, they can feel free to shop around for the best deal (whether it is the best price or the best service that they're after) with all the printers in their area. For convenience, PPG offers a handy, eco-friendly POD service for all small orders, which also allows authors to take advantage of PPG's online distribution services.

5. **Charitable giving to PPG Authors:**

    It is as important to lend others a helping hand once in a while as it is to help oneself, and PPG pledges to donate a minimum of 10 percent of its net profits earned through our Canadian authors each fiscal year in the form of a variety of publishing and/or writing grants toward supportive self-publishing packages for other aspiring Canadian authors. (Furthermore, as the company grows with more authors from other countries, we will look at similar region-specific granting programs for them, too.)

    Yet, that's not all. We want to give back to the Canadian economy as a whole; so, rather than keeping to ourselves all of the tax benefits of this type of donation, 20 percent of what we give will be "divvied" up among our paying Canadian authors (from that same fiscal year) as charitable donation and business expense receipts that they can use against their own Canadian taxes. Obviously, the amount we give will grow as we grow, and the recipient qualifications will be determined and modified along the way. For now, in our fifth year in business, we are offering a $3,500 publishing grant in the form of a contest that is free and easy to enter for any aspiring Canadian author from the age of 10 to 18 years old. Please refer to our Facebook page for details (Polished Publishing Group, 2013a).

Why Would You Want Support in Self-Publishing?

There are many great reasons why you should choose supported self-publishing ahead of "going it alone" with a vanity publisher–printer, but here are two of the most valued reasons: time and contracts. Do you have the knowledge and industry experience required to write all the applicable contracts for all your work-made-for-hire vendors (editors, designers, proofreaders, indexers, distributors, et cetera) in a manner that will ensure the protection of your copyright? If not, do you have the time and desire to research everything ahead of time only to turn around and have to write all these contracts yourself?

Did you know that many graphic designers, artists, and photographers assume they will keep the copyright ownership of whatever artwork they create on your behalf? Most authors are unaware of this, and they unwittingly agree to these terms simply because they didn't know that they should have had the conversation upfront or because they didn't put a proper contract in place with that vendor. By working with PPG, you will eliminate this problem altogether because we only hire artists who agree with our stance on copyright ownership: it belongs to the paying author. (This will be described in more detail in the copyright section of this book.)

One of the biggest benefits of allowing a company like PPG to be your personal project manager throughout the self-publishing process is that we already have all of the necessary contracts in place, and all of these contracts have been written to protect the copyright ownership of the self-publishing author. Another benefit is that we have already pre-screened all these people on your behalf. We ensure that they all have five or more years' experience in their respective fields. This is a benefit, so you can be assured that you'll end up with professional quality at the end of this publishing process—and that's what you want. You want professional quality if you expect to compete in the marketplace against other trade books and turn your own book into a reputable bestseller.

Another benefit to working with PPG is that we've been through this publishing process several times over, so we've fine-tuned it to ensure that it runs as quickly and seamlessly for you as possible—to get your book out to the public sooner than you could on your own. We negotiate on your behalf all of the contracts and take care of most of the administrative aspects of things on your behalf so that you can focus on the writing and marketing. This is a huge advantage because so much must be done, and the task can feel quite overwhelming and daunting along the way.

This is an emotional process, this book publishing business—for *every* author, male and female, without exception. Authors are already dealing with enough stress in the form of self-doubt, fear of the unknown, et cetera, without adding any extra frustrations into the mix. PPG's publisher was an author first, so she understands firsthand what authors are going through. Not only does PPG understand the various frustrations that come up throughout the process, but our team has also been trained to anticipate and manage them ahead of time. This is why our process has been set up the way it is. It is the very reason why we take the time to personally review the publishing contract, line by line, with each and every author to ensure that he or she understands it fully before we ever let him or her digitally sign that contract. It is the very reason why we created our publishing project timeline document to ensure that our authors (and our vendors) always know where they are in the process—and how their respective decisions will affect that timeline all the way through. (Everyone is given deadlines right from the start, and this helps the project to stay on track.) It is also the very reason why we send additional detailed instructions to our authors all along the way so that they always know what to expect from us next, in addition to what is needed from them. We're on top of it!

Do you have records management experience? No? Well, you're in luck because we do—and our knowledge in this area is yet another way that we can save authors a ton of time. PPG fully appreciates why it's so important to ensure that everyone involved in a project is following the same file-naming convention when saving his or her electronic files, and we use a standardized professional electronic filing system to help us better track each book project all along the way.

By doing things this way, we all have a consistent record of all the versions of the book, all along the way, which makes everything much more easily searchable and accessible in the event that we ever have to go back to check on anything (i.e., if the author questions changes that have been made). With a clearly thought-out records management policy and procedure such as this one, everyone knows exactly what to type in to search for a particular book rather than wasting valuable time trying to guess at file names.

All of these legal records (emails, saved files, et cetera) are very important because they are the paper trail that we all need to keep track of what's been done and to avoid any of the "he said, she said" types of disagreements that might arise along the way. Those types of things are major time and money wasters—and it's PPG's job, as a self-publishing author's professional project manager, to minimize (preferably eliminate altogether) all time and money wasters from the process. PPG will nip these kinds of things in the bud very quickly—professionally and tactfully, but quickly! So how does this benefit our authors? They can feel free to let us be "the bad guy" in these tricky types of situations, while they focus their efforts on more important things such as the sales and marketing of their books.

Do You Need an Agent? Do You Need a Publicist? What's the Difference?

To clarify, a literary "agent" is a representative whom authors hire to help them "flog" (sell) their unpublished manuscript to various trade publishers in the hopes they find one who will publish it for them. By contrast, a "publicist" is a representative whom authors or publishers can hire to promote the final published product to various wholesalers and retailers in the hopes that they will increase sales of that book.

After reading this chapter in full, it is clear that there is only one publishing business model in which you might want to hire an agent to help you sell your manuscript to a publishing company—trade publishing. It is an unnecessary expense in the vanity and supported self-publishing business models because, in those models, the likelihood of being published is already very high.

Publicists, on the other hand, can be useful in *all* situations—provided that you have the finances to cover their fees. You will be able to decide whether it is necessary as you read through this book and learn all the different ways that authors can successfully promote and sell their book themselves.

SECTION TWO:

Understanding Copyright

"Everyone has the right to the protection of the moral and material interests resulting from any scientific, literary or artistic production of which he is the author."

~United Nations, *Universal Declaration of Human Rights*

AN ELEMENTARY INTRODUCTION TO INTERNATIONAL COPYRIGHT

When it comes to copyright, four primary questions seem to arise most readily: What exactly is copyright? How do I obtain it? How do I protect it? How long does this protection last? This section of the book will provide an elementary introduction to international copyright (graciously written for us by Ian Gibson, Esq., an attorney who is licensed in the State of California) to provide aspiring authors with a solid starting point of reference that answers all of these questions *and* a couple more, including, "How does working with a publisher in another country affect my copyright?" As Gibson recommends, for those authors who wish to delve deeper into their own country's copyright laws or who require formal legal advice about a specific book project or publishing contract, please consult an experienced attorney licensed in your area.

WHAT IS COPYRIGHT?

Copyright is a form of protection provided to the authors of original works, including literary, musical, visual arts, and other intellectual forms of expression. Essentially, copyright gives the owner of an artistic work the exclusive right to use and to authorize others to use their work (e.g., reproduce, distribute, perform, display, prepare derivative works, etc.), subject to some exceptions.

HOW DO I OBTAIN COPYRIGHT OWNERSHIP OF MY WORK?

Copyright ownership occurs automatically as soon as an original work is fixed in a tangible medium of expression. For example, copyright ownership of these words is being created as I store them in my computer (i.e., "fixing them in a tangible medium"). Under widely adopted international treaties, no registration is required with a government body to own your creative expressions. However, significant benefits often exist for those who register their work.

How Do I Protect My Copyright?

Although copyright ownership is legally recognized as soon as an original creative expression is fixed in some tangible form (e.g., written down, saved to a hard drive, etc.), the owner of such a work can often gain significant benefits through the formal process of copyright registration.

To understand the benefits of registration in the context of protecting your copyrighted work, let's look at a hypothetical infringement scenario. If an author created and published a novel and later discovered that someone had copied the main characters, themes, plot points, and even some exact text, and published that content in another book claiming it as his or her own work, the law provides several remedies. The copyright owner could seek what is called actual damages and injunctive relief. Actual damages are a legal remedy based on the financial harm suffered by the copyright owner and the ill-gotten gains of the infringer. For example, if the hypothetical infringer sold $10,000 in PDF downloads, a court may order the infringer to pay that figure to the copyright owner. Injunctive relief is another legal remedy whereby a court issues an order for someone to do or stop doing a particular act. For example, an order could be issued requiring the infringer to stop all sales of the infringing book and destroy any physical copies in their possession.

Actual damages and injunctive relief are powerful remedies available to copyright owners. However, if this author had registered her literary work with the U.S. Copyright Office prior to infringement or within three months of first publication, she would have some additional remedies, including statutory damages and attorneys' fees. The remedy of statutory damages refers to a monetary award permitted by law. In the United States, 17 U.S.C. § 504 provides a range of $200 to $150,000 as an award for each work infringed, with willful infringers being potentially liable for the high end of that spectrum. An attorneys' fees award means that the prevailing party in a copyright infringement lawsuit can force the losing party to reimburse the winner's attorneys' fees. In other words, if this hypothetical author sued and won, the infringer could be ordered to pay the author's legal bills, which can total hundreds of thousands of dollars or more.

Although certain minimum standards for copyright protection have been adopted by virtually every developed nation, some significant differences exist under national laws. For example, neither Canada nor the United Kingdom requires timely copyright registration to have statutory damages available as a remedy for copyright infringement claims. Clearly, the requirements for statutory damages and attorneys' fees, among other things, vary from country to country, so I recommend seeking the counsel of an attorney licensed in your area for more information.

In addition to registering your work with the appropriate government authority, I recommend that authors place a copyright notice (e.g., "© 2014 Ian Gibson, Esq.") in a conspicuous location on their work. This simple act might serve as a deterrent to would-be infringers. Although formal copyright notice is no longer a legal requirement in many countries, it remains a best practice to put the world on notice of one's claim to ownership. It also helps to demonstrate that any infringers do so willfully despite the prominent notice of ownership.

In the event of a copyright infringement lawsuit, proving your creation of the work at issue and the date of creation is paramount. In the United States, for the reasons discussed above, no substitute exists for registering your work with the U.S. Copyright Office—which accomplishes these objectives. That said, the laws regarding registration and benefits thereof vary significantly by country. See Kim Staflund's earlier book, *How to Publish a Book in Canada . . . and Sell Enough Copies to Make a Profit!*, for more information on this topic for Canadians. Generally speaking, proof of your date of creation can be achieved effectively through a number of means via the Internet, by publishing the work through a third party like Polished Publishing Group, or, of course, by registering your work with the copyright office.

How Long Does Copyright Last?

Pursuant to certain international treaties, the minimum duration of a copyright is generally life of the author plus 50 years. If the work is anonymous or pseudonymous and, thus, the life of the author cannot be determined, the duration of the work will be 50 years from its publication or, if unpublished, its creation. In the case of applied art and photographic works, the minimum term is 25 years from the creation of such a work.

Many countries exceed these minimum standards. In the United States, for example, a work originally created on or after January 1, 1978, by a single author is ordinarily given a term for the author's life plus an additional 70 years after the author's death. For more information specific to Canadians, see Kim Staflund's earlier book, *How to Publish a Book in Canada . . . and Sell Enough Copies to Make a Profit!.*

How Does Working With A Publisher In Another Country Affect My Copyrights?

There is no international system of copyright protection. Typically, authors will follow the laws of the country where they reside—after all, this is likely where they primarily intend to market and sell their work. However, in today's hyper-connected marketplace, working with publishers, designers, and retailers, among others, often crosses national borders.

How does this affect your copyright ownership status? A select few forward-looking publishers, such as Polished Publishing Group, frequently work with authors around the world. Polished Publishing Group allows the authors that it works with to retain 100 percent ownership of all work (e.g., words and artwork) produced in connection with their book; therefore, these authors walk away from the process with full rights (which means they should typically follow the laws of the country in which they reside).

Unfortunately, not very many publishers follow this practice, and authors must do their due diligence before selecting a publisher. Hiring an experienced copyright attorney to review the agreement would be ideal.

At a minimum, I strongly encourage you to review closely any publishing agreement presented to you before signing it. If the language of the contract isn't clear regarding who owns 100 percent of your book, do not hesitate to ask for clarification in writing. If you do not, there could be serious consequences.

Is Quoting Another Author's Work In My Book Copyright Infringement?

Quoting the work of another writer might constitute the infringement of a copyrighted work. However, there are certain limitations and exceptions to a copyright owner's monopoly over the use of their work to allow for commentary, news reporting and other limited circumstances. These limitations are often referred to as a "fair use."

In the United States, the law sets out four factors to consider in determining whether the use of another's copyrighted work was "fair." Specifically, 17 U.S.C. § 107 includes the following factors:

(1)   the purpose and character of the use, including whether such use is of a commercial nature or is for nonprofit educational purposes;

(2)   the nature of the copyrighted work;

(3)   the amount and substantiality of the portion used in relation to the copyrighted work as a whole; and

(4)   the effect of the use upon the potential market for or value of the copyrighted work.

In the context of quoting a sentence or two or a prior work for the purpose of commenting on that work, the secondary use would almost certainly be a fair use. If the secondary text used large sections (e.g., entire chapters) of a prior work and added little in the way of commentary or criticism, these factors might lean towards that not being "fair" and, instead, constituting copyright infringement.

For information regarding best practices for quoting authors under Canadian law, see Kim Staflund's earlier book, *How to Publish a Book in Canada . . . and Sell Enough Copies to Make a Profit!*.

*** Ian Gibson, Esq. is an attorney who is licensed in the State of California. As with any general legal information, this document is no substitute for specific legal advice. If you have a legal issue that needs personalized attention, please contact an attorney. This document is for educational purposes only and is not intended to create an attorney–client relationship. This material may be considered advertising under applicable state laws.

COPYRIGHT SIMPLIFIED (UNDERSTANDING PUBLISHING CONTRACTS)

As the original creator of your manuscript, you own 100 percent of all of the rights to reproduce, publish, sell, and distribute your words in whatever manner you see fit. Your manuscript belongs to *you* and you alone—from the moment you write it. It is only when you decide that you want to publish your manuscript into book format with the hopes that you'll earn some money (or educate people, or entertain people, or whatever your personal reasoning is for publishing it) that the copyright ownership of that work might shift to someone else, depending on which publication method you choose. In other words, you might take a few different routes toward having your book published, and each of these book publishing methods affects your copyright ownership a little differently.

It is vitally important that you review a publishing contract in full before you ever sign it; and, if the contract before you is filled with a bunch of hard-to-understand legalese, then ask the questions you need to ask to ensure that you fully understand the agreement that you're about to enter into. Hold the company accountable for explaining it to you and putting you at ease. You have that right as one of their clients.

TRADITIONAL (TRADE) PUBLISHING

Some authors will submit their manuscripts to a traditional (trade) publisher for consideration in the hopes that it will be published free of charge to them. What they might not realize is that whoever is paying for the publication of a book is the one who owns the primary rights (the *copyright*) to that book. Trade publishers are business people who are buying a product to try to turn a profit for themselves, and that "product" is the copyright ownership of your manuscript (whether permanent or temporary—it varies with each contract). In this business model, writers usually retain only the basic publishing rights that recognize them as the author of the book and allow them to be paid a small percentage of the retail price in royalties (usually only up to 10 percent per copy sold). The trade publisher keeps the rest of the profits because the trade publisher owns the book. Thus, as the owner of the book, that trade publisher also reserves the right to sell off additional rights for additional profit down the road.

VANITY PUBLISHING

Authors who choose the vanity publishing route usually retain 100 percent ownership of their written words; however, if the vanity publisher has produced the cover artwork for them, (nine times out of ten, in my personal experience) that company usually retains the copyright of that artwork. This means that authors must always go through the vanity publisher to have their marketing materials and books printed.

A contract with a vanity publisher will usually also give that publisher *non*-exclusive online distribution rights throughout North America, the United Kingdom, Europe, and possibly the whole world. All this means is that the publisher reserves the right to sell and distribute copies of the book through its online channels (i.e., Amazon.com) for the duration of the contract; however, this is a non-exclusive contract; therefore, the author (and any other distributor designated by the author) is also free to sell copies of the book within those regions. If it were an exclusive contract, only the publisher would be allowed to sell the book online within those regions.

Supported Self-Publishing

Last but not least, authors can also choose to publish through a supportive self-publishing house like PPG where they will retain 100 percent copyright ownership of both their words and their artwork. That said, much like the contracts with vanity publishers, a contract with a supportive self-publishing house would also include non-exclusive online distribution rights worldwide for a specified term. This gives the authors much greater exposure without limiting their ability to sell wholesale author copies on their own wherever they choose to sell them.

Eventually, once you're selling lots of books and making a name for yourself with the general population, you'll begin to see the true value of retaining majority (i.e., FULL!) copyright ownership—because this is when more business people will come knocking and asking to buy additional rights to your book. Maybe someone in Quebec will want to purchase the exclusive French language rights to your title so he or she can be the only one to reproduce, print, and distribute it in French to that region's Francophone population for a profit. Maybe others will want to buy the exclusive North American film rights so that they can adapt the book for film in this region.

You can "divvy up" the rights to a book in so many different ways that it would be impossible to list them all here, but this gives you a very basic idea.

What are all these rights worth? In any industry, a thing is worth what someone will pay for it. It could be worth *millions* to the primary owner of the book, so it's a good idea to retain as much, if not ALL, of that ownership as you can right from the start. Then, when the movie producers and foreign publishers start calling, hire a copyright lawyer to help you determine the best price for each sale of rights to each different buyer.

Who Owns the Artwork?

In addition to my book publishing background, I also worked in the world of print advertising sales for many years. What these two industries have in common is that each business (be it a newspaper, magazine, telephone directory, or book publisher) creates artwork for its respective clients as part of its overall service offering.

A company's artwork policy can vary: some companies believe that once you've paid for and published a creative work, the copyright belongs to you and you can reproduce it at your discretion as part of your own marketing campaign. Other companies believe any artwork that they have created for you belongs to them and can only be reused with their permission at an additional charge. Having been on both sides of this coin—as both the service provider and the paying client—it is my humble opinion that the copyright for a creative work belongs to the paying client, and that all of the high-resolution artwork should be returned to that client upon receipt of payment. I won't delve into any examples related to print advertising here, but I will discuss my own personal experience with book publishing.

Each time I write a new book, I tie it into the preceding book(s) by including graphics of my past book cover(s) at the end of the story along with an updated author bio. (Alternatively, in the case of *this* book, those graphics are included in the back matter as well as being scattered throughout the body.) I also reproduce this promotional copy on my author website and printed flyers. This helps me to sell my older books (back list) along with my most current book (front list) at signings and various other events.

On one particular occasion, I wanted to create a large poster with all my book covers included on it. I intended to use this as an eye-catching display at a high-traffic craft sale. Great idea, right? Unfortunately, one of the book publishing companies through which I had published refused to release a high-resolution copy of my book cover to me so that I could have this poster printed locally. "We own it," they said. "It belongs to us." Without the high-resolution file, I was unable to blow the image up large enough for the poster. The smaller file they sent to me was useless to me.

It seems to me that this is a "nobody wins" scenario. This company wasn't keeping my artwork under lock and key with the intention of ever using it itself. The company was simply keeping it to prevent someone else (me) from ever using it elsewhere. In other words, it was forcing me to use only its restrictive, non-customizable marketing services alone. I found this very frustrating as a paying customer who needed something a little outside that company's scope of services at that time.

Due to this personal experience, I founded PPG with the philosophy that self-publishers are not only entitled to 100 percent copyright ownership of their written words, but they are also entitled to 100 percent copyright ownership of the artwork that our vendors create for them. (After all, the authors are paying for the production of their books, right?) Rather than storing their print-ready cover and interior files ourselves, we return everything to our self-publishers (working files, finished files, everything). This enables our clients to print extra copies of their books wherever they choose to, and it allows them to produce top-notch marketing materials at their discretion. To me, this is an "everybody wins" scenario because, each time they display their book covers with one of PPG's logos on it, it helps to promote them, the designer, *and* PPG. That's how it should be, wouldn't you agree? At the end of the day, I would rather have customers return to PPG because they *choose* to return because they had a good experience— never because they feel forced to return.

SECTION THREE:

Book Sales
and Marketing

"People don't buy for logical reasons. They buy for emotional reasons. . . .
Stop selling. Start helping."

~Zig Ziglar

DO YOU OFFER THE BEST VALUE OR THE BEST PRICE?

Presumably, you bought this book because you want to know how to present yourself as an industry expert in your field by publishing a professional-quality book that you can sell commercially. If this is the case, you need to start thinking about the sales and marketing aspect of book publishing long before you even finish writing your book. This is why the Book Sales and Marketing section of this book lands before the Modern Book Publishing Process section. It's that important to your overall success.

First and foremost, it is crucial to understand that nobody and nothing can be everything to everyone; so, you must think about what you represent (what the core intention of your book truly is) and who your customers are long before you put the whole package together. Authors need to ask themselves: Do I offer the best value in my field or do I offer the best price? Who is going to want to read my book and why? What are their personal principles? In other words, what do they appreciate most when they're looking for this particular thing that I'm selling? The best value? Or the best price?

For those of you who personally rate price ahead of value or who automatically assume that everyone else does, think again. There are many different people in this world with many different needs and reasons for buying various books. If you want to reach a certain demographic, you must understand their motives and market to them very clearly and consistently. In other words, once you've determined what you represent (which should match what your desired clients desire most), you now must ensure that your entire marketing strategy—from the wording inside your book to the design of your cover to the price tag you've attached to every version of that book—is consistent across the board. Make a clear decision early on about who you are and to whom you are selling the book, and then be true to that vision through and through.

When To Sell Based On Value, Not Price

Both types of marketing have an appropriate time and place. However, most people are already pretty comfortable with price-based selling (i.e., offering sales and discounts to try to undercut the competition's price); therefore, we're going to focus on value-based selling here, instead. It's an important skill to master because, at the end of the day, *anyone* can sell on price. But here's the biggest problem with that plan: if price is the only thing you've got, and then someone else with a similar offering comes in at a lower price than you can match, you're done. You're *finished*. You've got nowhere else to go. However, if you can learn how to sell based on perceived value right from the start, you'll always be able to justify your price as it is. You can even increase that price down the road by adding even more value to your overall offering.

Here are a few examples, in various contexts, intended to illustrate the point that it's sometimes better to sell based on value rather than on price.

The Food Industry

Sometimes, when people go out for dinner, they just want a fast, cheap hamburger at a fast-food restaurant—they're in a rush, they're hungry, they're craving beef, and they just want something on the go that doesn't cost too much. Other times, those same people might want to go out for dinner and enjoy a gourmet hamburger. It's all beef, right? So why would anyone be willing to pay more for one burger than the other? It's because sometimes they desire better service and a more relaxed, enjoyable dining experience at a higher-priced restaurant. Also, that gourmet burger was prepared by a professional chef who has years of experience preparing artistic, delicious food—and that experience commands a higher price!

On that note, if you went out to a high-priced restaurant, expecting to purchase a gourmet burger, and that burger was marked as "on sale" and priced the same as a fast-food burger, would you not question the quality of the beef? Case in point: If you say that what you're selling is valuable, and you wish to position yourself as an expert in your field, whatever you're selling—whether a burger or a book—should be priced to reflect that value. The price should be consistent with the very clear message that you are trying to send; otherwise, people will question it and probably purchase elsewhere.

The Moving Industry

Let's say that you are the director of the Records Management Department at a large corporation that has recently acquired another company. Your job is to hire a professional mover to transfer all the newly acquired confidential files from their current location to your offices downtown. You publish a Call for Tenders in your local newspaper to see what offers come in.

One offer comes in from a local moving company that positions itself as always having the best price. Other than that, all it has to offer is a free estimate, guaranteed delivery date, and both local and long-distance relocations for businesses and residential clients.

However, a second offer comes in that is more than triple the price offered by the standard moving company. This mover positions itself as a leader in the records management industry with over sixty years' experience in moving confidential files for all types and sizes of business clients. The primary mandate is to protect the confidentiality and integrity of every client's files. Every employee who works for this company must undergo and pass a criminal check, plus they are all put through a rigorous training program to ensure that they have a strong understanding of records management, retention, and classification schedules before they are ever allowed to touch a client's information. File moves can be managed in whatever way best suits the client (i.e., if it is important for the client to be able to access these files at all times throughout the move, this can be arranged). Finally, this mover will not only move all of the records, but it will also do a file conversion at the same time so that all of the files from the old company are labeled in the same way that files are labeled at the new company, ensuring continuity in all the information, making it easier and more efficient for employees to find it when they need it.

As the director of the Records Management Department at a large corporation who values confidentiality, efficiency, and continuity of information above all else, which of these movers would you be most likely to choose? (I don't think I have to tell you that this client went with the second, higher-priced mover.)

Sometimes price is the most important thing in the moving industry. However, sometimes value and security is more important. It all depends on the type of move being done. As with every other industry, it is important to know your customer before you create your marketing strategy, and then to make sure that your price is consistent with that strategy. This will ensure that you make the sale because your customers will be more apt to trust what you're telling them.

The Book Industry

Let's say that an aspiring author wants to self-publish a professional-quality, bestselling ebook that can stand proudly beside a trade-published bestseller. He decides to buy an ebook written by someone else on the topic to educate himself about the industry.

The first ebook he comes across costs only $3.99. It is titled *How to Self-Publish an eBook Quickly and Easily!* He scrolls through the first couple of pages to review the content of the book and notices quite a few typos riddled throughout. There are bad breaks, widows, and orphans everywhere. Also, important components are missing from the book, such as a bibliography stating the legitimate sources of important sales statistics and claims. The primary message of this book is that it's easy to publish an ebook quickly and cheaply, and there's no need to invest in a professional copy editor, designer, or proofreader to help produce it.

The second ebook he comes across costs $19.99, and it is titled *How to Publish a Bestselling eBook*. He scrolls through the first couple of pages to review the content of the book and notices how much more polished and professional this book appears. All the proper components of a professional-quality book are included. He notices, in the author's biographical sketch, that this book was written by a professional writer and book publisher with over twenty years of experience in sales, marketing, and book publishing. In addition, in a whole section of this book, the author discusses various ways to market and sell ebooks to customers.

Which book is this aspiring author going to buy? Keeping in mind that his primary goal is not only to publish an ebook, but to publish a bestselling ebook; he will most likely go with the second, more expensive example. In this case, value is more important than price.

A Skydiving Example

In his online blog entry, *Sell Based on Value, Not Price,* Robert Plank (2013) provided yet another perfect example of a time when value is definitely more important to a customer than price:

> "Let's say you went to the store and saw two parachutes, side by side . . . one looks okay and costs 50 bucks. The parachute next to it looks HALF as good and costs 25 dollars. Which one do you choose?
>
> The 'regular' $50 one, right?
>
> Then you notice there's also a 100 dollar parachute on the shelf. It comes with an extra emergency backup chute, a checklist for what you should check for before jumping out of an airplane, and a DVD with skydiving tutorials. You also get one free skydiving lesson included . . . and one free issue of 'Skydiving Magazine.' (Ok I'll admit, I've taken this analogy way too far.)
>
> NOW which parachute would you go for . . . the regular one or the fancy one?
>
> You might be able to get by with the regular parachute, but you'd feel a lot better if you had that checklist, the DVD, the magazine, and the lesson.
>
> People will pay more for handholding. Don't try to sell the smallest amount for the lowest price, try to sell the most USEFUL stuff for the highest price."

Do you see? Although price is a consideration for some people in some situations, oftentimes, customers buy depending on perceived value first. If that weren't the case, we wouldn't see any BMWs on the road, would we? Nor would we see so many people walking around with Venti Lattes from Starbucks in their hands when they could just as easily pick up a coffee from Tim Hortons or Dunkin' Donuts. The same principle can be applied to books as can be applied to cars and coffee—and everything else you're trying to sell.

These are merely a few examples of the times when value might be more important to a customer than price. There are many more examples, as I'm sure there are many more examples of times when price takes the lead. The point here is that it's important to evaluate your customers ahead of time—to understand what they appreciate most—before determining how you will market your book to them. Also, once you've determined what your marketing strategy will be, it is crucial to set your price to match that strategy. Consistency and clarity of your message is the key if you wish to have long-term success in selling.

How To Price An eBook

As a preface to the next part about how to price an ebook properly, I will say that pricing a digital book is a wee bit different from pricing a physically printed paperback book. A little later on, we're going to discuss the logistics behind determining the best retail price for a paperback book, depending on where it will be printed and where it will be sold. We can't even discuss it at this stage because it's impossible to guesstimate one's printing costs without knowing the final page count of the finished book; likewise, it's impossible to set a profitable retail price for that book without knowing one's printing costs.

All that said, many authors incorrectly assume that consumers make ebook buying decisions according to different criteria than their paperback buying decisions—that it's based solely on price ahead of value because of the format of the book. They mistakenly suppose that the ebook version of a book should be priced cheaper than the paperback version because of its reduced production costs (i.e., no printing involved). This is a flawed premise because, again, all kinds of different people in this world have all kinds of different motives and reasons for buying ebooks.

Some customers buy ebooks based on price:

- They prefer downloading ebooks to their laptop, desktop computer, or ebook reader, that they received as a gift, because ebooks are cheaper to buy than paperbacks or hardcover books.

Some customers buy ebooks based on value:

- They bought an ebook reader for all their ebooks for the convenience of having them all in one place (i.e., so they don't have to cart around lots of heavy books with them).

- They see significant value in the content of the book (i.e., it contains priceless information and instructions that can help them to earn more money or to better themselves and their lives in some measurable way).

- Going paperless to help save trees is more important to them than saving money.

- They want to have the latest technology in their hands before anyone else has it. (These people will almost always pay more to stay one step ahead of other people.)

These are just a few of the reasons why people might buy ebooks. There are probably many more. It all comes back to what I stated earlier about the importance of consistency in one's overall marketing message. If consistency is the key, shouldn't the ebook version and paperback version of a book be priced the same? If it's the *content* of the book that the client is buying and if that content could potentially help them to improve their finances or health or some other aspect of their lives in a measurable way, isn't that worth the same to them no matter what format they're buying it in? The answer is yes. Absolutely!

Why Kindle Is Best for Price-Based eBook Marketing

Amazon's Kindle Direct Publishing (KDP) platform allows publishers and "indie" authors to upload interior book files specially formatted for their e-readers; and it has a generic, front-cover-generator option available in cases where the client hasn't already had one designed. This is a prime example of the vanity book publishing model in that vanity publishers promote themselves as the fast, cheap, and easy self-serve way to "publish" (but let's call it what it is . . . *format*) a book without any mandatory professional editing, design, proofreading, et cetera, involved whatsoever.

Like many other vanity publishers, Amazon's Kindle does its best to maintain control and ownership over the files uploaded to its site by enticing authors into an exclusivity contract via its KDP Select program. In addition, Amazon controls every Kindle eBook's retail price point (ebooks *must* be priced at $9.99 or *lower* with zero room for negotiation) and will only allow authors to connect their POD paperback books with their Kindle eBooks online via their "Kindle MatchBook" option so long as that ebook is reduced to as low as $2.99 per copy (Amazon, 2014a, 2014b).

It will likely take you forever to make back the money it cost you to *properly* publish your book if you set your retail price at $2.99 per copy. Not only that, but such a low price truly devalues your content. When you price a book that low, what you're telling people is, "This is a cheap book full of cheap content." It is what it is.

Kindle's KDP platform not only prices ebooks very low, but it also allows authors the choice of offering their books free of charge for two to five days out of every 90-day period to try to bolster new readership (Amazon, 2014c). Here's a rhetorical question for you: Would you pay for something from an author whom you know will turn around and offer it free of charge to you for two to five days out of every 90-day period? (Isn't there some old adage in this regard . . . something about why bother buying the cow when you can have the milk for free?)

There *is* an acceptable time and place to hand out free copies of one's book (please refer to the Complimentary and Promotional Copies and Review Copies sections of this book for details). Otherwise, a much more effective way to entice new readers into buying your book is with a "Sneak a Peak" option that allows them to look inside your book to read a small portion of the content for free. But giving away the *whole* thing for free? No! Especially not *thousands* of copies of your book all at once!

Obviously, if you're trying to sell your book based on value rather than price, the Kindle platform defeats your purpose with a price point set that low and a marketing platform that encourages giving books away for free. For those selling based on value, it's best to sell your books elsewhere.

Why Kobo Is Best for Value-Based eBook Marketing

Luckily, various other ebook retailers out there will happily sell several ebook formats for their clients without exclusivity contracts, while also letting those publishers determine their own recommended retail prices. Kobo is one of these retailers. When you upload your files to Kobo Books, you can set your own retail price from the start (albeit, they can put the book on sale if they choose to, as it is with all retailers across the board). Nobody at Kobo will dictate that the primary retail price must be a certain price or lower with zero room for negotiation.

On that note, for the avid Kindle authors out there who believe that a book sold online can only become a bestseller if it's an ebook that is priced low or given away free of charge, think again. The digital POD paperback version of my book, *How to Publish a Book in Canada . . . and Sell Enough Copies to Make a Profit!* (978-0-9864869-6-8 on Amazon), became an Amazon.ca bestseller only a short month and a half after it was first published. The recommended retail price for that book is $19.99 USD. It reached bestseller status using the various online marketing techniques described in this book—not because of its price. (Ebooks and the ebook format that PPG chooses to produce for our authors will be described in more detail later on in this book.)

Do you offer the best value? Or do you offer the best price? Decide who you are early on—what the core intention of your book truly is—and then be true to that vision through and through. Understand your target market—your customers' preference—*before* you design your sales and marketing strategy, and then make sure that that strategy is consistent with their preference in every single way, including the retail price that you've set for every format of your book. You'll sell far more books over the long run if you do this.

We'll discuss specifics on how to set the retail price of a *paperback* book a bit later on; however, even before authors have all the information that they need to do that task, they should clarify their vision first. They can then factor that vision into their pricing strategy to ensure consistency of their message across the board.

Sell The Benefits Of Your Book—Not The Features

Customers don't buy books so much because they want a book. They buy books because they want a solution of some kind. Marketing campaigns that focus on selling the features of a book ahead of the benefits make the incorrect assumption that their readers will automatically understand why they should buy it. Proper communication of the benefits is crucial to make a sale.

- **Here's a common example of the difference between features and benefits:**

  This line tries to sell the features of a new pair of gloves: "Buy our waterproof, breathable, soft-shell work gloves today!"

  This line sells the benefits of those features: "Keep your hands warm and dry while maintaining ease of movement during your entire outdoor work day!"

The first advertisement focuses only on the features of those gloves and assumes that potential customers will understand how a "waterproof, breathable, soft shell" can benefit them. However, what if those customers have just moved to Canada from a tropical island, and they have yet to experience a humid, winter climate? What if they haven't worn gloves to do outside handiwork before now? How will they understand the true benefits of these particular features unless you spell them out to them ahead of time? Those customers might not realize it yet, but they aren't merely buying a pair of gloves—what they're buying is the ability to do their job outdoors as comfortably and easily as possible.

- **Here's an example related to a non-fiction ebook:**

    This line tries to sell the features of a new ebook cookbook collection: "Our new ebook cookbook collection contains a wide variety of favourite family recipes for busy moms!"

    This line sells the benefits of those features: "Now busy moms can enjoy peace of mind and some extra spare time with this vast collection of favourite family recipes all stored together in one compact, easy-to-find place!"

What busy mom couldn't use some peace of mind and extra spare time? Also, wouldn't it be nice to have all of her favourite family recipes quickly accessible to her in a sleek, new digital ebook format rather than having to search through several tattered, old cookbooks to find what she's looking for?

When you're thinking of ways to sell your cookbook, remember your customers aren't merely buying recipes from you—what they're buying is the ability to care for their families (and themselves) in as easy a way as possible. On that note, some readers might not recognize the true benefit of buying an ebook ahead of a paperback in this situation unless it is spelled out for them. I'd also be willing to bet that a busy mom would pay a good dime for the convenience (perceived value) of having all her recipes together in one searchable ebook file, so this is a prime example of a time when authors can definitely set their retail prices a bit higher. ($45 for one ebook cookbook that replaces over $350 worth of tattered, old cookbooks? Fair deal? I think so!)

- ### Here's an example related to a fiction paperback:

     This line tries to sell the features of a new paperback fantasy novel for adults: "This new paperback fantasy novel contains over 250 pages of action and adventure as Harold the Great treks through the magical world of Myth."

     This line sells the benefits of those features: "Curl up on your couch with the quiet comfort of this paperback fantasy novel tonight. Escape from reality into Harold the Great's magical world of Myth—and feel all your stresses melt away."

Some people still love the way a good paperback novel feels in their hands, and they'll buy one over an ebook any day. Grab their attention with a really solid, compelling benefit statement. Appeal to their emotions by reminding them why they love to read paperback fantasy novels so much. It works! It will coax them into buying almost every single time!

HAVE YOUR ELEVATOR PITCH READY TO RECITE AT A MOMENT'S NOTICE

When you sit down to design a marketing strategy around whom your customers are, what they value most, and how your book best meets their needs, begin by writing down a list of your book's features, but don't stop there! Dig a little deeper to determine the benefits of those features to consumers. That extra time and effort will make a world of difference to your sales for a couple of reasons: first, it will make for some persuasive back cover copy that will draw readers into buying the book; and second, it will give you a quick and easy *elevator pitch* to recite to anyone you run into who asks about your book on the spot (The Free Dictionary, 2013). It's your chance to sell it without them even having read that back cover copy.

What is an elevator pitch and why should every author have one memorized and be ready to recite at a moment's notice? An elevator pitch is a brief sales pitch that clearly outlines the features and benefits of your book: "The name 'elevator pitch' reflects the idea that it should be possible to deliver an elevator pitch in the time span of an elevator ride, or approximately 30 seconds to two minutes" (Wikipedia, 2013b). When delivered correctly and confidently, it can result in a sale right on the spot. That's assuming that you're carrying one or two of your books with you at all times—which, of course, you are because you're an entrepreneurial sales dynamo!

INCLUDE A CALL TO ACTION IN ALL YOUR MARKETING MATERIALS

Now that you have your riveting back cover copy written and you've memorized your gripping elevator pitch, you basically already have everything you'll need to include on websites, posters, and advertisements designed to promote your book. There's just one more thing you'll need to include in all of your marketing materials: a call to action. Here are a few self-explanatory samples you might choose from:

- Click here to buy a copy!

- Buy this book today!

- Get one while supplies last!

- Why wait? Pick up your copy right now!

Simply stated, a call to action is your very clear request to consumers to buy your book TODAY! Right now! In fact, don't just build it into all your marketing materials and advertisements; build it into your elevator pitch, too. Sometimes, salespeople do an amazing job of convincing buyers that whatever they're selling is a wonderful thing, but then they let those buyers walk away without actually asking for the sale while the opportunity is still hot. Don't let that opportunity get cold! Come right out and ask for the sale right in the moment. It doesn't work all the time, but it works a lot better than not asking at all—that much I can promise. If you get used to doing this, you'll sell way more books over time.

TRADITIONAL SALES TECHNIQUES

There are so many different ways and places to sell a book these days that it's mind-boggling. You're no longer limited to selling books at home, either.

You can quite easily sell them worldwide if you want to! Here are a few examples of some traditional sales techniques you might consider when it comes to selling your book. We'll follow these up with some great online sales techniques, too.

Media Tours

A media tour is a series of interviews with newspapers, magazines, and broadcast stations to promote you and your new book. Tying in a media tour with a book signing is a great way to increase traffic to the event. These types of interviews can also be used as leverage to convince various retail outlets to carry your books: "I'll mention your store during my interview if you'll agree to sell copies."

You don't have to be J.K. Rowling to stir media interest. All you need is a good angle. For example, if you're from Toronto, you might want to promote yourself as an "up and coming Toronto author" to the media in that city. Alternatively, if you've published an historical fiction or non-fiction work about a particular region, you can contact the media within that region for an interview.

Once you reach J.K. Rowling's level of renown, a press release with a one-liner such as "Announcing the latest release by . . ." is about all you'll need to generate buzz and arrange interviews for yourself anywhere in the world. Until that day comes, placing a personal phone call to request an interview in your own neck of the woods is a good start and is usually much more effective than any press release, fax, or email alone.

Whom do you contact to book an interview? It varies depending on the media: you'll want to talk to the book review editor when contacting a newspaper; your best bet is the news editor at a radio station; and you should ask for either the producer of the morning show or a community events reporter at a television station.

Each time you complete an interview, it's a great idea to ask for a copy of it so you can continue promoting it even further. For example, you can scan a copy of a newspaper article to display on your blog; or you can ask for copies of your radio and television interviews in a YouTube-compatible file format and then post them to your YouTube channel. Please visit the Polished Publishing Group YouTube channel for an example.

There are many cost-effective ways to sell more of your books—from readings, to signings, to craft sales, to speaking engagements. A timely media tour can complement all of these events to make them even more successful.

BOOK SIGNINGS

Not only is it possible to move a surprising amount of books at a signing, but it is also a great way for a new author to get used to being "on display" in public. A book signing doesn't have the same pressure to perform and entertain as a reading. A book signing is a much more comfortable arena to learn how to talk about (sell) your book to readers.

Although each bookstore does things a little differently, the process for setting up a book signing is fairly standard. It's a matter of contacting the store's event coordinator to arrange a mutually available date (Saturdays are often best for retail traffic) and to provide consignment copies of your book to them ahead of time. Sometimes, they charge a basic fee to cover co-op advertising. In this instance, both the author and the bookstore agree to pay 50 percent for any ads that are placed to promote the event. Other than that, the only investment is your books (which, presumably, you already purchased beforehand) and your time (signings generally last for two to three hours during an afternoon).

The bookstore will set up a display table for you ahead of time. From there, it is up to you to engage customers in conversation and to convince them to buy your book. You sign it for them and then direct them to the bookstore's checkout to pay for it. When the event is over, the bookstore will send you the payment for your portion of the profits (which is typically 60 percent of the retail price). The bookstore might choose to keep additional consignment copies of your book on hand if they feel that they have a good chance of selling them, or they might return any leftover copies to you.

To improve the success of your signing, it's a good idea to do your own self-promotion rather than to rely solely on bookstore traffic. One way to generate buzz is to post event notices in community newspapers and on as many nearby bulletin boards as possible. Of course, there is no substitute for inviting your friends and family members to these events. (I can always count on my mother to buy up half the stock in one fell swoop!)

If you personally invite all of your colleagues, friends, and family members in the area to your signing, you can expect to have a successful book signing and sell from 20 to 30 books (or more, depending on how many people show up) during one event. If you neglect to invite anyone, and you rely solely on bookstore traffic, it is common to sell only one or two books during one event. Inviting people and promoting the event yourself makes a significant difference.

Book Launches

When I worked for a small literary publisher several years ago, I used to help organize book launches and readings for our writers in celebration of our new releases. In cases in which the author was established and had a large following, we could justify a solo event knowing we'd recoup our costs in book sales. For the newer authors, we would often celebrate with a group event. This was not only a cost-saving measure for us, but it also helped to relieve fledgling performance anxiety by allowing these new authors to share the spotlight with someone else.

As a self-publisher, you are charged with organizing your own celebrations just as a traditional publisher would do for its authors. If you're confident you'll be able to sell enough books to cover the full cost of an event, you're in an enviable position. If not, I recommend selling tickets to your reading and advertising the event with as many display ads, community listings, bulletin boards, and websites as you possibly can in addition to inviting your friends and family members.

When you envision a book reading, do you see an early evening, wine-and-cheese affair in a quaint little bistro? Can you imagine yourself relaxing with a drink in hand, going from table to table to greet each of your guests until it's time to take centre stage and read from the first chapter of your book? This common option comes to mind for many artists. Depending on whether you choose a cash bar to fund all the drinks, it may be a quite a costly option.

How about a breakfast launch? Many restaurants have private dining areas that are ideal for events like this. Buffets are a great way to satisfy all of your guests' tastes in an economical way. Once everyone is satisfied, relaxed, and enjoying his or her morning coffee after a fine meal, you can take your chair to the front of the room, sit down in front of your guests, and begin reading from your book. This type of setting is particularly suitable for authors of children's books who might have underage guests attending the launch party.

Next to the venue, your only investment for a book launch is (a) your books (which, presumably, you already purchased beforehand); (b) your time (time to sell tickets and to organize the event, plus three or four hours for the event itself); (c) your presentation (anything from a simple table cloth to display stands to a cash box); and (d) your cash float (so you have change available for paying customers). A fair amount of work is involved in organizing an event like this, so you might want to enlist the help of volunteers to sell tickets and books on your behalf. Or you can always hire the staff at PPG to help you for a fee.

Much like a bookstore signing, the amount of books you will sell at a book launch depends on how many people you invite and who shows up. Try to give people enough notice, and arrange it on a day that is conducive to the largest number of people being able to attend (i.e., a Saturday or a Sunday on a regular weekend as opposed to during business hours or provincial or state holidays). That will increase your chances of success.

COMMUNITY CRAFT FAIRS AND FARMERS' MARKETS

One relatively inexpensive way for a new author to sell books is by reserving a table at a community craft fair or farmers' market. Your only investment is (a) your books (which, presumably, you already purchased beforehand); (b) your time (craft fairs generally run from around ten o'clock in the morning to three o'clock in the afternoon on a Saturday); (c) your table registration fee (which is usually somewhere between $35 to $50 depending on the venue and location); (d) your presentation (anything from a simple table cloth to display stands to posters); and (e) your cash float (so you have change available for paying customers). That's all there is to it.

The number of books you can sell at these venues is largely dependent on traffic flow. How well did the organizer promote the event on behalf of the vendors? How well did *you* promote your own attendance at the event? (It's not only up to the organizer to bring people to the sale!) It can be "hit or miss" at these fairs, but don't let that discourage you. If you were able to hand out a few flyers or business cards to people who wouldn't otherwise know you, that's still valuable exposure for a new artist. Also, if you sold more than enough books to pay for your table, consider the event a success.

How much of an entrepreneur are you? Rather than paying to attend someone else's community craft fair, have you ever considered organizing one of your own? It's a lot more work, but it's a way to earn extra profit in addition to your book sales. First, you find an available venue and decide how many tables it will accommodate. Next, you figure out the total cost of that venue plus any other advertising you will use to promote the sale (such as display ads in community newspapers, street signs for the day of the event, and Facebook event invites to name a few). Finally, you divide up your cost per table (which should include an additional fee to cover your own time and effort as the organizer) and start selling the event to other vendors. In my experience, most people will jump on the opportunity to promote their products and services at such a reasonable rate. Once you get one or two people interested, the word spreads fast and the tables are all full before you know it.

TRADE SHOWS AND CHRISTMAS FAIRS

In my last book, *How to Publish a Book in Canada . . . and Sell Enough Copies to Make a Profit!*, I discussed my personal experience and observations sharing a booth with one of PPG's entrepreneurial authors at the 2012 Spruce Meadows Christmas Market in Calgary, Alberta. I met a couple of different authors who returned there year after year, earning profits on both their front list and back list titles year after year, and had my own expectations regarding how much profit one could earn from book sales at Christmas markets and trade shows *completely* blown away. I now know that it's possible for a single author to see a *profit* of $3,000+ at one show in book sales alone (and that's *after* taking the cost of printing the books and paying for the booth out of the equation).

I learned that 2012 was one of these authors' eighth year at the Spruce Meadows Christmas Market, and he'd seen a profit every single year. To give you an idea of how many books you'd have to sell to make a profit at Spruce Meadows . . . well, the cheapest booths there cost $1,100 each at that time. Many of them were even more than that. So, if your book is priced at $12 retail, for example, and it costs you $2 per unit to print it, then you're earning $10 per book. You'll have to sell 110 books just to break even on the cheapest booth in the place. From my own experiences, I'll admit that I was skeptical that anyone would be able to sell that many books at one Christmas market, but this author proved to me that it's possible to sell even *more*! Moreover, most impressive of all, he proved that it could be done year after year with one's so-called back list titles!

What's the key to success in sales at any trade show or market? Have fun with it, first and foremost. Be approachable and friendly to the people who walk by your booth. But every good salesperson knows that it takes much more than a radiant personality to draw people into a booth. Make sure that your walls are adorned with eye-catching pictures related to the book you're selling so that you can attract from far away the people who are interested in that particular topic. Have some free giveaways on your table in the form business cards and bookmarks promoting your current and upcoming books. Make it enjoyable—not merely for them, but also for *yourself.* People can unconsciously sense the energy of others around them, and they'll be attracted to the more pleasant energies of those who are clearly enjoying being there to share the day with them. And once you get them into your booth, ask for the sale using your polished elevator pitch describing the various features and benefits of your book. *Close the sale* right then and there.

Another important piece of advice is this: it isn't enough to get yourself to every venue that will let you in to sell your book such as the various markets, trade shows, and fairs. You must also ensure that the venues you choose will bring an audience that matches the audience you are trying to attract with your book. For example, an auto show might be a great place to sell a book with a strong male audience, whereas books tailoured toward a female audience might sell well at The Woman's Show.

"THINK OUTSIDE THE BOOKSTORE" AND GET INSIDE OTHER RETAIL OUTLETS

In today's competitive retail marketplace, authors sometimes need to "think outside the bookstore" to move larger quantities of their books. Sometimes, placing a book in a different retail outlet altogether will help it to stand out more.

Books by Jack Canfield, for example, get the prime real estate in a bookstore—right in the line of sight, in the highest traffic areas—because they are guaranteed to sell. Unfortunately, most unknown authors must compete for attention from an obscure shelf in a small section of the store. The only customers who might find their books are the ones specifically visiting that section and taking the time to browse it thoroughly. Understandably, this makes it difficult for the majority of newcomers to earn a decent profit from bookstore sales.

How Bookstore Retailing Works

To compound matters for new authors (self-publishers in particular), the majority of traditional bookstores prefer to buy titles marked as "returnable" by a publisher or distributor. This provides them with an out for any books that don't sell. They can clear them off the shelf and return them for a full refund, making room for the fresh, new releases after a couple of months. Books are sometimes returned a bit scuffed or worn down, depending on how often they've been handled. At times, they even have the bookstores' stickers still attached. Now authors are left with an unsalable second-hand product and no royalties to show for it.

For new authors, bookstore sales often work best in conjunction with a book signing because such an event allows authors and their books to appear front and centre if only for an afternoon. Many books can be moved this way, especially if the author is naturally social and willing to engage customers in conversation. As well, the bookstore sells the books on a consignment basis, which means no returns! Everyone wins!

How Chain Store Retailing Works

When I worked for a small Canadian literary press years ago, one of our most entrepreneurial authors—the author of a mystery series for children—had a wonderful idea. She approached several gas station chains located in various small towns along the Saskatchewan highways, asking them if they would like to sell her children's books at the till along with the various other magazines and comic books. They thought it was a great idea because many families always dropped in to get gas and take breaks during their long drives to and from the city, and many of their children bought comics to keep themselves occupied in the backseat during these trips. She sold a lot of her wholesale author copies this way and probably made much more money than she would have made just relying on her publisher royalties. I always smile whenever I think about her. I have always remembered her. What an inspiration she was—and *still* is—for Canadian authors everywhere.

These days, most (if not all) large retailers require their merchandisers to obtain licensee liability insurance and fill out some paperwork before they will allow them to put up any displays anywhere in their stores, never mind near the till. The same applies to authors, but this extra bit of effort might well prove lucrative in the end. If it takes a title from an obscure bookstore shelf and places it on a display rack facing a high-traffic aisle, it might just sell more copies. It's definitely worth looking into.

Some of the retail chains new authors might consider selling their books in are gas stations, drug stores, department stores, mall kiosks, et cetera. The key is to stand out by being placed in as high-traffic an area as possible because this will attract new sales from impulse buyers who happen to be walking by. Why do you think grocery stores place chocolate bars and magazines at the front, right by the till? No one goes to a grocery store intending to buy chocolate bars and magazines. They go there for groceries, but everyone has to walk by the till . . . and, oh, those chocolate bars look good! Don't they? And that news story in that magazine sounds pretty intriguing, too. Might as well pick up one of each! Authors can take advantage of human nature in much the same way that other companies do.

On that note, for all the very good reasons to sell books *outside* a bookstore in all the various venues mentioned in this chapter, there is one very important instance when an author will want to stick with a primary bookseller: when that author wishes to be recognized as a bestseller.

WHAT CONSTITUTES A BESTSELLER? HOW DO I BECOME A BESTSELLER?

The above two questions are intertwined because, to become a bestseller, you must first understand what actually constitutes a bestseller. Once you know the answer to that question, you must do four things to achieve it:

1. Write a saleable book (all the while keeping in mind your target market and the best way to communicate with them, as discussed earlier).

2. Have the book professionally published (so that those in the traditional publishing sector such as booksellers, reviewers, distributors, and the like will take your book seriously).

3. Become familiar with the rules of the game in your region pertaining to bestselling books.

4. Respect and follow those rules when selling your books.

"Lather, rinse, and repeat" in every marketplace that you wish to make your book a bestseller—a particular bookstore chain, perhaps an online ecommerce bookseller such as Amazon, and so on and so forth.

In *How to Publish a Book in Canada . . . and Sell Enough Copies to Make a Profit!*, we looked at what constitutes a bestseller in Canada—what has to happen for authors to be recognized as a national bestseller on an official published bestseller's list in that country. We also discussed the caveat here: that you cannot put the label of "National Bestseller" on the cover of your book until it has been recognized as a national bestseller on an official published national bestseller list.

In this book, we're going to briefly discuss what constitutes a bestseller on an online ecommerce site such as Amazon because so many of us are now selling our books worldwide using this retailer. There are some similarities to the traditional rules, and there are some differences.

Amazon's system for determining who lands at the top of one of their bestselling lists is as complex and ambiguous as Google's algorithm for which websites will land at the top of a keyword search. It's different from traditional bestseller rules in the sense that it's determined by online sales that are tracked by computers' IP addresses in various regions versus being tracked by physical book sales in bookstores. But it's similar in the sense that its bestsellers are determined by who sold the most books during a certain time period versus who sold the most overall. It's like a competition: whoever sold the most books in this allotted time period is the winner, the bestseller, for this time period.

On Amazon, the time periods are broken right down to hour-long increments per category as shown in the below illustration:

So long as your book remains in the top 100 sellers for that category, it will remain on the bestselling list in the category each time Amazon refreshes the list (hourly). For example, I first noticed my book on the bestseller list in three applicable categories in November of 2013, one and a half months after it was first published:

When I checked again a couple of months later, it had risen to the top ten in two of the categories and it was in twelfth place in a different third category. It continued to fluctuate up and down like this for several months:

Now that we've identified what constitutes a bestseller on Amazon, let's go back to the second part of the question: How do I become a bestseller? Well, honestly, you can have some fun with this! Get entrepreneurial about it! Let your inner salesperson run a little wild! Here are three simple examples from an unlimited list of ideas that you might consider:

1. Was your book written to supplement your business in some way? Then you might consider writing the costs of publishing, printing, distribution, and advertising for this book into the business plan you've written to obtain a business grant or loan. Repetitive, consistent advertising (whether online, in print, on television or radio, et cetera) carefully directed toward your target demographic group (and directing them to buy your book on Amazon on a particular day) will help to create top of mind awareness for your book in the same way that it does for a business. This will get your title noticed by both readers and the major booksellers alike, which, in turn, will increase your sales and might just help you sell enough copies to turn your book into a bestseller in more than one market.

2. Similarly, crowdfunding is a relatively new way of generating revenue to fund special projects without having to pay back small business loans with interest. If it can work for any business venture, it can certainly work for an author. Check out websites such as Cookieejar, RocketHub, and Indiegogo for inspiration and ideas.

3. How about advertising a "$100,000 Book Launch Celebration!" on your blog and taking out a specialty insurance policy (which usually only costs a couple hundred dollars) to offer a chance at a grand prize of $100,000 for every copy of your book that is sold during a particular five-hour period on Amazon? How much fun would that be? Promote the event to enough other people on your social media sites, and I'm willing to bet you'd stir up some interest in your book from all kinds of new customers you didn't bank on beforehand. I'll bet you could sell a couple hundred books—maybe even more—by doing this.

The possibilities are endless when you think like an entrepreneur—when you get creative and make sales something fun rather than something painful. It's the difference between simply publishing a book and publishing a PROFITABLE book—a BESTSELLING book! Once you're recognized as a bestseller on a *published* bestselling list, and you can put those words "Bestselling Author" on your book cover beside your name, then you'll be taken that much more seriously as an author which will create even more momentum toward continued book sales in the future. Everyone who buys books wants to buy a bestseller. Make sense?

Still feeling a bit resistant to the idea of selling yourself? Want some help creating an effective sales plan for your book? Well, PPG happens to know some talented, innovative, and ethical salespeople who LOVE to sell (crazy kids!) and would be honoured to help out a PPG author—for a fee, of course, because they are salespeople, after all. Something to keep in mind.

ONLINE SALES TECHNIQUES

For as many traditional ways and places as there are to sell your book, there are just as many—if not even more!—online sales techniques you can use to promote your book to whomever you want to, all around the world, by using the benefit of technology and keyword searches. To best use this technology to promote and sell more books, every author should have a Web presence and they should do what they can to direct as much online traffic to that page as possible on a daily basis. Here are but a few of the many ways one might achieve this feat:

BLOGGING FOR SEO: SEARCH ENGINE OPTIMIZATION

The primary reason why blogging is so important is *search engine optimization* (SEO), which means to improve (optimize) your standing in the search results on search engines such as Google, Yahoo, and Bing. Think, for a minute, about when you use a search engine to find something. Where is the first place you look when the search results come up? The top and centre of the page? In addition, how many links are you willing to click through to find what you're looking for? Maybe ten at the most? Maybe your eye will scan down that first page for something interesting; or, if you have the time, maybe you'll dig a little deeper and look through the second or third page to see what comes up there. Statistically, most people will stay on the first page. This is why it's crucial to make sure you appear on that first page for as many of the major keywords that are associated with your product or service as possible. Regular and consistent blogging is one way to help you achieve this.

For example, Polished Publishing Group (PPG) publishes all kinds of books from fiction to poetry to non-fiction business books. We know our clientele often "Googles" phrases like "how to publish a book" and "business history books" to find our types of services, so we make sure to write blog entries and online articles with these key words in them and link them all to our website. Here are the results of doing so:

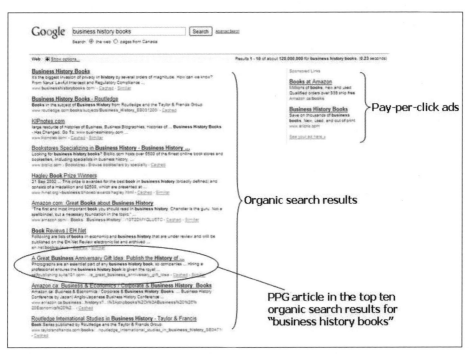

With the help of blogging, PPG appears on Google's first page of organic search results for one of our primary key words: "**Business History Books.**"

You can use two forms of blogging (also known as "online writing for SEO") to promote yourself: online articles that are written for and posted on high-ranking online publications and blog entries that are posted to your own website or blog site. Each has its own unique advantage.

Online Articles (Online "Advertorials")

You might have a fairly high search engine ranking for *some* of your keywords (i.e., your business name, your book's title). Blogging can help to improve your ranking for *all* of them. The idea is to write several keyword-rich articles—500-word essays that contain the phrases that your customers type into a search engine when they are looking for your products and services—and then share those articles with others via email and social media websites. The ultimate goal is for your articles (and, eventually, your website) to show up in the top five search results on page one of a search engine because this will dramatically improve the chances of someone clicking on them and making a buying decision on the spot. Obviously, the more articles that are posted online on a regular basis, the more momentum will be built, and the better it will work. This type of blogging has a cumulative effect, meaning that it will drive more traffic to your site over time.

Online articles should have an editorial appeal to them that matches the criteria set up by the online publication to which they are being posted. Their primary purpose is to educate people about a certain industry or topic.

To view samples of these types of articles, visit online publications such as EzineArticles.com and Examiner.com. Better yet, visit EzineArticles.com/?expert=Kim_Staflund and www.examiner.com/writing-in-calgary/kim-staflund. Here, you will see example articles specific to the book publishing industry.

Search engine ranking is based on a complex point system known as an algorithm. The higher your points, the higher you land in the search results. Each online advertorial is like a webpage in itself and can garner higher points for your own website with two of the major criteria search engines are looking for: backlinks and traffic. Backlinks are clickable referrals from one relevant webpage (an online advertorial) to another (your website). The more backlinks to your website, the higher its point value will be in the eyes of a search engine—especially if those backlinks are coming from relevant, high-ranking, online publications like EzineArticles.com and Examiner.com. It also stands to reason that more backlinks equate to more traffic over time via the people who are redirected to your website by clicking on them.

Blog Entries

Blog entries are a wee bit different from online articles in that you can say pretty much whatever you want, however you want to say it, because you are posting it to your own page instead of someone else's. Blog entries can be an obvious advertisement for your products, services, events, et cetera, if you choose. You aren't limited by anyone else's content criteria.

A blog site can be a website in its own right, or (for businesses, in particular) it can be an extension of one's primary website. For example, PPG's primary website is www.polishedpublishinggroup.com. This is where our customers go to buy book publishing packages from us. The PPG Publisher's Blog is an extension of our primary website: blog.polishedpublishinggroup.com. This is where PPG's founder and publisher blogs and answers industry FAQs (frequently asked questions) about the book publishing industry. Upcoming PPG webinars and workshops are also promoted here.

Blog entries improve your search engine ranking, depending on another major criteria that search engines are looking for: quantity of posts. Google's algorithm rewards more points to websites that post new and relevant content on a regular basis. As it stands today, three to four new blog posts per week is optimal in the eyes of a search engine.

BLOGGING IS WORD-OF-MOUTH ADVERTISING ON STEROIDS!

Blogging is a fantastic way to reach more potential buyers more quickly than ever before. Many people, particularly small business owners with fixed budgets, find that word-of-mouth advertising is the best form of advertising for them. This might well be true. When people hear good things about a company from someone they know and trust, they are more apt to trust that company upfront and check it out for themselves.

The only issue with verbal word-of-mouth advertising is that sometimes things get "lost in translation" along the way. Many of us can relate to this by remembering a game we played as children. A dozen or more people sit in a circle together, and a phrase is whispered into the ear of the first person who then whispers it to the next, who then whispers it to the next, and so and on, and so forth. By the time that the last person hears the phrase and repeats it aloud for all to hear, it has a completely different context than it did when the first person heard it. With verbal word-of-mouth, word can spread like wildfire, yes—but sometimes the message is distorted along the way.

Blogging, on the other hand, is a written form of word-of-mouth advertising, which means the original message remains intact. Rather than simply speaking about your message, it's the Share button at the bottom of an online article or blog entry that enables readers to share your message with others via email and social media websites such as Facebook, Twitter, and LinkedIn to name a few. Imagine that! Imagine how many people are currently using Facebook, Twitter, and LinkedIn alone—never mind all the other social media sites that are out there today. Imagine how quickly a message can be spread to so many others with the simple click of a Share button!

Possibly the greatest benefit to blogging is that it is an unobtrusive and cost-effective form of advertising. Where traditional advertising methods (e.g., newspaper, television, radio, and billboards) try their best to "interrupt" customers into noticing them, blogging appeals to the audience that is already in the market for your products and services. No need to try to interrupt anyone to gain his or her interest; if he or she is typing in those keywords to try to find you, it's because he or she is already interested in what you have to offer. All you have to do is to be there in the top organic search results and, voilà: you've got your prospective customers' attention and hopefully some new business to go with it.

INCREASE ONLINE TRAFFIC BY *TEN TIMES* IN ONE MONTH USING SOCIAL MEDIA

Don't believe that it's possible to increase online traffic to a webpage by TEN TIMES in one short month using blogging combined with social media marketing? Let's start with the visual proof first. Then we'll talk about how you can emulate the same results.

Back in 2010, I created an alfresco video reading to promote my third book online. At the same time I posted that video on PPG's YouTube Channel, the company that helped me to produce the video also posted it on their own YouTube Channel. I took it a step further by promoting my YouTube link on various social media sites, my company blog, and a couple different online publications. The other company didn't. It was a wonderful experiment that provided us with quite astonishing results:

Webpage That Was Posted but *Not Promoted*: **23 Views** in One Month

Webpage That Was Posted and **Promoted: 229 Views** in One Month

That's the indisputable power of blogging and social media marketing at work. Every time I post a new blog entry, video, or online article for my books or my publishing company, the very next thing I do is to share that link on Twitter, Facebook, LinkedIn (including various groups on LinkedIn), Reddit, Digg, StumbleUpon, Mixx, and Multiply (to name a few). The entire process takes about half an hour of my time—and the results? Well, they speak for themselves, don't they?

Not enough time in the day to do your own blogging and social media marketing? We understand. That's why PPG has a team of qualified online SEO writers who can help. Keep that in mind.

Create a Facebook Author Page to Promote Yourself and Your Books

It's probably unnecessary to go too deep into an explanation about what Facebook is and how to use it because almost everyone in this country (in this world!) now has a Facebook account of his or her own if he or she has a personal computer and Internet access. The fact that it gives people the potential to reach an audience all around the world makes it a powerful advertising vehicle. The fact that it is free of charge makes it easy for anyone and everyone to use.

The beauty of Facebook is the freedom that it gives to each individual to determine how much of their own information they wish to share publicly. You can set up your personal timeline in all kinds of different ways. For example, you might want to keep your timeline fairly private so that only your approved Facebook friends can see your personal posts and information. However, you can create a separate public page that is accessible to everyone for viewing whatever product or service it is you are trying to promote.

Facebook is not only a great place for a company like PPG to promote itself. Writers can also create their very own author pages to promote themselves, their books, and their upcoming events. Creating a page is free of charge just as creating a timeline is; and one can also set up a Facebook pay-per-click advertising campaign from that page if one so chooses. This plan allows for more robust and targeted online advertising. Visit the Polished Publishing Group Facebook page for more ideas and inspiration.

Be Sure to Tweet Your Author Events on Twitter

Consider Twitter the abridged version of Facebook. It is a great place to post brief comments or links to your online events and blog entries. (Each post you make is known as a "tweet" on Twitter.) This is all the rage in online marketing these days. Everyone is tweeting! You should be, too! Never before has it been easier to reach a global audience so quickly—not to mention free of charge. Your only investment is your time (unless you have someone else tweeting for you, of course).

The whole idea behind Twitter is to use the power of word-of-mouth advertising by getting as many people to follow you as possible, and you start this process by beginning to follow others first. According to *USA Today* bestselling author Julie Ortolon (2013), who is a strong advocate of Twitter, "When you post a tweet, it goes only to the people who are following you. If, however, your followers 'retweet' (RT) or 'reply,' it goes to all of their followers as well. Both these actions help you build followers. So, your goal is threefold: notify your followers about an event, get more exposure through RTs and replies, and gain more followers."

Another way to gain followers and attract people outside of your list of followers is by including hashtags in each of your tweets. A hashtag is to Twitter what a keyword is to blogging. For example, the keyword phrase "Canadian Book Publisher" could be formatted into a hashtag that looks like this #CanadianBookPublisher. When you include a hashtag like this as part of your tweet, your tweet will show up in all searches performed for those keywords on Twitter. It might entice even more people to view your profile and eventually begin to follow you, too.

Do these two things on a regular basis on Twitter, and the next thing you know, you'll have hundreds of Twitter followers who are subscribed to receive your tweets on a regular basis. The more regular and consistent your tweets are, the greater your top of mind awareness becomes among potential new customers just as it is with traditional advertising. Visit the Polished Publishing Group Twitter page at @PPGPublishing and my personal Twitter page at @KimStaflund for more ideas and inspiration on the types of tweets you might want to create to promote your business and your book.

Build a Strong Network on LinkedIn

Think of LinkedIn as Facebook for business professionals. Where your Facebook timeline is used to provide personal updates to your friends and family members, your LinkedIn page is intended to provide business updates to your colleagues and network with other potential business associates. This is where you post your professional resume if you're looking for a job or wish to highlight your expertise within your current field. Much like a Facebook page, you can set up events (i.e., for book signings) free of charge and invite all your LinkedIn connections to attend. What a great place to promote a new book to people who might not otherwise be aware of it!

On LinkedIn, you can join groups that are related to your field and you can promote your online articles within these groups. It's a great way to generate more traffic to that article—traffic in the form of people who have already shown an interest in your topic by virtue of the LinkedIn group you met them in. This is yet another way you might just make a sale.

The best way to understand LinkedIn is to start using it if you aren't already. Create an account. Then look at these two pages for inspiration on how you might build your own business and personal pages: Polished Publishing Group (PPG) | LinkedIn and Kim Staflund - Canada | LinkedIn.

Sell More Books Using Eventbrite

Eventbrite is yet another fantastic website you can use to promote upcoming events. One added bonus is that you can also use it to manage your mailing lists and ticket sales for those events. Another is the Event Affiliate Programme:

> With the affiliate program tool, event organizers can create an event-specific affiliate program for their event. This enables event organizers to increase attendance to their event by offering a referral commission to third-party promoters. The payment can be either a fixed dollar amount or a percentage of the ticket price—it's entirely up to the event organizer. Eventbrite gives event organizers and their affiliates all the tools they need to send, receive and track traffic, as well as keep track of commissions. (Eventbrite, 2013)

What better way to encourage other people to spread the word about your event for you while helping to sell more tickets!

Do a search for "Polished Publishing Group (PPG) on Eventbrite" to see how we're using our page. It might provide you with some ideas and inspiration for your own.

Post a Video Reading on YouTube

According to Wikipedia (2013e),

> YouTube is a video sharing website on which users can upload, view and share videos . . . to display a wide variety of user-generated content . . . including movie clips, TV clips, and music videos, as well as amateur

content such as video blogging and short original videos . . . . With its simple interface, YouTube made it possible for anyone with an Internet connection to post a video that a worldwide audience could watch within a few minutes.

Best of all, it is free of charge to both watch and post videos on YouTube. This is very good news for authors everywhere!

How Can Authors Use YouTube to Promote Their Books?

Wikipedia (2013e) went on to say,

> One of the key features of YouTube is the ability of users to view its videos on web pages outside the site. Each YouTube video is accompanied by a piece of HTML, which can be used to embed it on a page outside the YouTube website. This functionality is often used to embed YouTube videos in social networking pages and blogs.

In other words, YouTube enables authors to share their video readings with others via email, on social networking sites such as Facebook and LinkedIn, plus their own blog sites. Never before has it been so easy and affordable to reach such a broad audience so quickly.

That said, how about filming an alfresco reading to promote all the wonderful things about your book and your city, province, or state at the same time? Then how about posting that reading on YouTube for others to enjoy? The author of this book did just that and invites you to visit the Polished Publishing Group YouTube page to view it for inspiration on how you might do a video of your own.

How Long Should an Author's Video Reading Be?

When choosing a chapter or series of poems to include in their video readings, authors should keep in mind that the shorter the file is the better. There are two primary reasons for this: (a) it is easier to hold the attention of one's audience for briefer amounts of time, so a smaller video will improve the chance of others watching it to the very end; and (b) YouTube limits video uploads to ten minutes in length and 2 GB file sizes for standard account holders.

Which Software Program Do People Need to Watch a YouTube Video?

Adobe Flash Player, which is a common installation on most personal and business computers, is all that is needed to view YouTube videos. If, for some reason, a computer does not already have this software, it is easy to find a free download of it by doing a Google search for "adobe flash player free download" and then manually adding it to one's computer.

PAY-PER-CLICK ADVERTISING CAMPAIGNS

Pay-per-click (also sometimes referred to as cost-per-click) advertising is yet another tool authors can use to drive more traffic to their websites. Whereas simply opening up an account on sites such as Facebook, Twitter, LinkedIn, Eventbrite, and YouTube is free of charge, pay-per-click campaigns cost money. For anyone wishing to supercharge their *gratis* social media advertising, they might wish to complement their blogging with a targeted pay-per-click campaign.

The cost of a pay-per-click campaign depends on a few different factors:

1. Where is it being run (i.e., Google, Facebook, or LinkedIn)?

2. What region is it being targeted to (i.e., one province or state, the entire country, the entire continent)?

3. For how long does the campaign run (i.e., for a specified amount of time, or until a specified advertising budget has been used up)?

Although Google pay-per-click campaigns are designed to target specific keywords that users might type into the search engine (two example keywords that PPG has used in the past are "How to Publish a Book in Canada" and "Canadian Book Publisher"), Facebook campaigns are designed to target a specific Facebook demographic such as "female users aged 20–40" or "all users" who have expressed an interest in "book publishing," for example. When you start a pay-per-click campaign, you agree to pay X dollars per each click on your ads that are redirected to your specified landing site (hence the term "pay per click"). The landing site can be your website, an online article or blog you've written, a YouTube video you've posted, the webpage on Kobo or Amazon where your book is currently for sale, or whatever else you want to direct traffic to at that moment. That landing site is as crucial to your success as the pay-per-click ad is. Although the ad itself needs to contain an enticing enough message to make people want to click on it, the landing site to which they are redirected should contain a strong call to action that allows them to buy your product or service right then and there. That's the key! Ask for the sale and there's a good chance you'll get it!

Online publications (e.g., EzineArticles.com and Examiner.com) use the power of pay-per-click advertising to drive more traffic to their websites, but they take it a step further. They have arranged partnerships with various search engines to display their pay-per-click ads on the articles within their publications that have matching keywords. The search engine pays them a portion of the pay-per-click proceeds for any of the clicks that come directly from their articles; and they, in turn, share a small portion of those proceeds with the authors of the articles. This is another great reason for authors to do some blogging in the form of online advertorials. It's an opportunity to earn incremental income, while promoting your products and services and directing more traffic to your site.

To gain a better understanding of how pay-per-click works and how much it costs, contact the websites mentioned earlier. Ask them about their own pricing structures and policies. Each of them is a little different.

One final tidbit of marketing advice related to keywords and pay-per-click: incorporate your top search engine keyword into the title of your book, and voilà! A major bookstore might just place an eye-catching sponsor ad on Google that directs traffic straight to your book inside their store! I was surprised when I came across this! Talk about valuable free advertising!

(We'll talk about the importance of your book's title in even more detail a bit later.)

Where blogging improves your organic search engine placement, adding a key-word savvy book title into the mix might also provide you with some free pay-per-click visibility!

Paid Online Book Reviews

Different types of book reviews are available to help authors sell more books: unpaid traditional book reviews, and paid online book reviews. We'll discuss unpaid traditional book reviews in more detail a little later in this book; but, it's worth mentioning paid online book reviews in the sales and marketing section of this book for two reasons:

1. They can aid you in your efforts to direct traffic to the webpage on Kobo or Amazon where your book is currently for sale, thereby increasing the SEO for your book's title and your author name from there.

2. They can create more interest in your book on these webpages by actually posting the review right to the book for you, to let other potential buyers know they liked it. This may help increase sales on that site.

ForeWord Reviews (2014) words it well when they say:

> Book reviews are critical to getting your title noticed in today's overcrowded publishing space. Booksellers, librarians, and discerning readers depend on unbiased reviews from a trusted source to help them discover compelling new books. Objective reviews are the key. Book-buying professionals do not pay attention to 'likes' or softball testimonials on author pages.

Although you're *not* guaranteed a review when you send a book to a traditional book reviewer, you *are* guaranteed a review when you pay for one from a non-traditional book reviewer. That said, it would still be an unbiased review . . . which may be good or bad. Once the review is complete, you are given an opportunity to decline or approve it to be published online for all to see. If you decline it, you won't get your money back; it simply won't be shared publicly at your request. But if you approve it, it might be posted to the reviewer's high-traffic website, posted to your book online, and/or shared with various wholesalers and retailers all around your country (and possibly other parts of world, depending on where you have the book reviewed).

You can begin to see the importance of putting a book through the entire *proper* professional publishing process once you realize the value that a book review (particularly one posted online) can bring to your marketing campaign. On that note, let's take a detailed look at that publishing process now.

The Modern
Book Publishing Process

"Happiness does not come from doing easy work but from the afterglow of satisfaction that comes after the achievement of a difficult task that demanded our best."

~Theodore Isaac Rubin

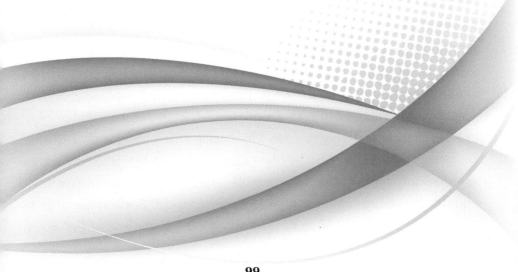

BOOK PUBLISHING FROM CONCEPTION TO PUBLICATION

Several little odds and ends are involved with the professional book publishing process—some obvious, others not so obvious. PPG has created the following checklist to help supported self-publishers keep track of what they will need in terms of supplies and what sorts of things must be done all along the way.

SUPPLIES YOU WILL REQUIRE

To publish a book in this day and age, you must have access to a properly functioning computer, email, and the Internet. You must also have a working knowledge of and access to a Web browser (such as Internet Explorer or Google Chrome) and software programs such as Microsoft Office (primarily the Word, Excel, and Picture Manager modules) plus Adobe Acrobat Reader. This will enable you to review and manipulate the various files that will go between you and the editor, designer, indexer, proofreader, et cetera, all through the publishing process. It will also allow you to communicate properly with the supportive self-publishing house regarding these files.

The good news is that the above-mentioned programs are pretty much standard on all PC computers these days. In other words, most computers you buy (whether desktops or laptops) usually come equipped with Internet Explorer, Microsoft Office, and Adobe Acrobat Reader. It's all usually built right into the price of the machine.

It is important not only to have a properly functioning computer, but also to have an up-to-date model to ensure that you can easily view the versions of files that are sent to you. That is, most vendors and publishing houses are now using Office 2010 with .DOCX file extensions that are unreadable to someone who is trying to open them using Office 2003 with .DOC file extensions. A publishing house like PPG can try its best, within reason, to save files into formats that are readable by earlier versions of Office (i.e., 2007) to help out its authors with older computers. PPG will always do our best to help with these types of things; however, at the end of the day, a book publisher is a book publisher—not an IT specialist—so we can only do so much. It is every author's responsibility to ensure that he or she is using as current and functional versions of software and hardware as possible.

WRITING YOUR BOOK

You can hire one of PPG's experienced ghostwriters to write your story in collaboration with you, or you can write it yourself. Either way, whether you write your story or have someone write it for you, it must be completed in Microsoft Word (MS Word). A bit later on, we'll discuss why it must be written in MS Word and how it needs to be formatted before submitting it for publication. Before that, we'll discuss some of the challenges you might encounter when writing a book on your own versus hiring someone else to write it for you, plus we'll show you how to handle those challenges as they arise.

Three Great Tips for Overcoming Writer's Block

Writer's block is a reality for many writers who are writing their own books. So how do you deal with it? What is the best way to finish writing a book? Should writers schedule a chunk of time each day and force the story out, or is it best to work only when the mood hits? These are common questions that many authors face at the prospect of finishing a book.

The truth is, starting a book is the easy part. The first few paragraphs or chapters can seem to flow out of an author's mind faster than her hands can type. This is the most enjoyable stage because it stems from impulsive inspiration, meaning that she is writing only when the mood hits. Unfortunately, if that mood doesn't hit on a regular basis, writer's block can easily set in.

Creativity is similar to muscularity in that it will begin to atrophy with a lack of regular stimulation. Just as even the finest athletes have those days when they must dig a bit deeper to find the will to continue on, all writers will have the same experience. On that note, the best cure for writer's block is discipline and perseverance.

Schedule Regular Writing Intervals

The best solution is to treat a book project like a regular job. Writers should set aside a certain number of hours each week and ensure that they are seated at their desks on time. By scheduling regular writing intervals in this way, writers can move past that fleeting impulsive inspiration toward a more lasting thoughtful inspiration and finish their books once and for all. Sometimes, when settling down to write, they might have no idea what they're going to say—and that's okay. It might take half an hour to get that first awkward sentence out and "unlock the floodgates" of creativity; but most authors are pleasantly surprised with how much they have at the end of the session. It's because the intention to create is the very thing that attracts the creation. That's the power of deliberate, thoughtful inspiration.

Set Target Dates

Another way for writers to stay on track is to set achievable but strict deadlines for themselves. Perhaps, in January, they might say, "I want the first draft of this book completed by the end of November." From there, they should guesstimate how many pages the book will be and break down the number that must be written per month, per week, per writing session to meet that page-count goal. Then stick to that schedule. Keep that self-promise. Just as intention attracts creation, persistence builds momentum.

Read Regularly

The writers who spend even as little as half an hour per day reading another author's work often find that they are more creative during their own writing sessions. It doesn't have to be another book; it can be an online article, magazine, newspaper, or blog. Sometimes, the least likely source can inspire the greatest creativity. The most important point here is that writers should keep themselves open and aware of the infinite pool of ideas all around them. Whatever it takes to get that first sentence out. From there, thoughtful inspiration can—and will—take care of the rest.

WORKING WITH A GHOSTWRITER TO WRITE A BOOK

Although some authors are both qualified and have the time to write their own books, others might choose to hire professional ghostwriters to help them create that compelling narrative. Both are acceptable ways to produce a book. That said,when hiring a ghostwriter to help pen a book, it is important for authors to remember that ghostwriting is an ongoing, collaborative process (much like the entire publishing process); and, to make things run more smoother, they should have a few things prepared ahead of time.

Preparation of Clear Deadline Expectations

Before contacting a ghostwriter with a new book project, it is important for authors to set a clear goal regarding when they would like to see their new book in print. Even more crucial: that deadline should be shared with the ghostwriter at the very start of the partnership. This will ensure that both parties are headed in the same direction at the same time.

Is this a business history book that must be published and printed before that centennial celebration in July? Is this a special cookbook or novel that the author wants available in time for Christmas gift giving? These are two examples of critical deadlines that must be shared with the ghostwriter ahead of time. From there, the ghostwriter can backtrack, with the help of the project manager (publishing house), to determine how much time is available for the writing, editing, design, proofreading, indexing, and printing stages of the book publishing process to meet that deadline.

Preparation of Notes

Book publishing is done electronically in this day and age; therefore, it's necessary for all author notes to be prepared in MS Word format ahead of time. If a ghostwriter is supplied with an unorganized set of notes that are scrawled on several different sheets of paper, the author's costs will immediately skyrocket because it will take the ghostwriter extra time to type everything into MS Word from scratch. By contrast, if authors supply all their notes to the ghostwriter in one continuous MS Word document, it will be much easier to follow and to begin writing the content within the same file. This is a huge time and money saver.

The top of this document should include a first draft outline of roughly where the author wants this book to go and in what order he or she wants each section to appear. From there, the ghostwriter will ask more questions to gain a clearer picture of the author's vision, and the book will begin to take form.

Mental and Emotional Preparation

Some authors go into the ghostwriting process with the misconception that, once they've handed their notes to the professional, their job is done and the book will be written. It is important to understand that ghostwriting is an ongoing, collaborative process in which the author will be required to answer questions and proof chapters all along the way.

Authors can also expect to go through a series of emotions during the ghostwriting process. It is natural to feel an initial resistance to each new draft—to feel a bit frustrated if things aren't worded exactly the way the author first envisioned. This is a natural reaction during the ghostwriting process, particularly when it comes to personal books like biographies. Recognizing this, authors should read a draft over once, and then put it away for a couple of days to give their emotions time to settle. If they do this, it will be easier to read it over again, the next time around, with a more objective mindset. In that objective state, they can then feel free to change the words they don't like or correct the dates, times, and names however they see fit. All authors make better decisions in the objective state than they do in that initial emotional state.

Analogy for Ghostwriting

A big part of a police officer's job is to write reports—to try to interpret the recollections of various witnesses and to create the most accurate appraisal of a situation as possible. The biggest challenge in writing this report is that although each witness saw the same thing, they'll all tend to give the police officer a different account mainly because each of them was viewing it from a different vantage point. An officer can only take what he or she is given and translate it as factually as possible.

Ghostwriters have a similar challenge when it comes to interpreting the notes they receive from authors and trying to turn those words into a veritable yet readable, marketable story. Sometimes, the ghostwriter might interpret some things a bit differently than the author initially intended. That's okay. It can all be fixed along the way, which is why we say that this is an ongoing, collaborative process—just as the entire supportive self-publishing process is. It is a partnership from start to finish.

If authors can keep this analogy and these tips in mind throughout the ghostwriting process, they will be more patient with it, which will make it run much more smoothly for them and their writing partner. In the end, they'll come out of it with an amazing book of which they can both be very proud.

PROTECTING YOUR COPYRIGHT

It is up to you the author–self-publisher to protect your own copyright before you send your book to any book publisher. Please refer back to the copyright section of this book for instructions on how to do so.

OBTAINING A PUBLISHING QUOTE: CHOOSING YOUR BOOK PUBLISHING PACKAGE

Once your manuscript is written, and your copyright is protected, it's time to figure out your publishing costs. Some authors prefer to do their own cost calculations by leafing through PPG's pre-set publishing packages and à la carte services in the Book Publishing Services section of the PPG Online store: http://shop.polishedpublishinggroup.com. Others prefer to receive a quote by email. Either way, to determine the total cost of publishing your book, you'll need the following information:

What Is the Total, Final Word-count of Your Manuscript?

You can find the total, final word-count of your manuscript on the left-hand bottom corner of your MS Word file. A publisher needs this figure because the editor, proofreader, and indexer fees are all calculated on a per-word basis.

PPG highly recommends that each author include the entire front matter, body, back matter, and back cover copy of their manuscript inside the MS Word file that he or she submits for publication. This way, the book is professionally edited and proofread in its entirety to ensure consistency in style (grammar, punctuation) all the way through. This is one of those important distinguishing details for the authors who want the most professional result. Trade publishers edit and proofread their authors' book covers and interiors in full. Self-publishing authors should do the same.

How Many Graphics Will Be Included in the Interior of Your Book? How About the Cover?

A graphic can come in many different forms: it might be a photograph or a drawing made by an illustrator or a table that you created in MS Word that now must be saved as a JPEG so it can be properly transferred into the designer's graphic design software. The more graphics you want included within your manuscript and book cover, the more work you create for the graphic designer. More work equals more time, which translates into more costs all around. This, too, has to be factored into the price of publishing a book.

PPG automatically allows for up to ten interior graphics and two cover graphics within all our publishing packages. Anything over and above that will cost a little extra per graphic.

Will Your Book's Interior Be Colour or Black and White?

Did you know that if even just one letter—even one small dot—of your interior is done in colour and the rest is black and white, it is still considered a colour interior by printers? Colour interiors cost a bit more to print than black and white interiors. They also take a bit more time to design depending on how much colour is desired and how much colour correcting the graphic designer might have to do along the way. As such, PPG's colour publishing packages are a bit more expensive than the black and white publishing packages to factor in these costs.

What Trim Size Will Your Book Be?

One of the most common trim sizes is 6 x 9 inches. This means that the front cover is six inches wide by nine inches tall. Standard trim sizes such as 6 x 9 inches will cost less to print because they require less manual work (e.g., additional trimming) at a print shop. This book is a 6 x 9-inch trim size. This author's new age fiction books, on the other hand, are all 5.5 x 8.5-inch trim sizes—another standard measurement in books.

Maybe you have a different vision for your book. Maybe you want it to be squarer. Or maybe you envision it larger or smaller. Whatever the case may be, it is important to include your book's expected trim size in your publishing quote request because the trim size is another factor in your costs down the road. The more unique the trim size, the more manual work is involved for both the graphic designer and the printer. On top of that, today's POD printers are still somewhat in their infancy and cannot necessarily handle all the possible trim sizes that an offset printer can handle. In other words, the authors who want their paperback books to be available on ecommerce sites such as Amazon will be limited to the various trim sizes that a POD printer is equipped to handle. PPG quotes on these types of projects on a case-by-case basis because technology is always changing and upgrading, so the available trim sizes might change along with it.

Submitting Your Manuscript

How writers submit their manuscripts to a book publisher depends on the type of publisher they are working with. The first rule of thumb is to visit the publisher's website to review their submission guidelines before submitting anything to them. If their guidelines state that they prefer to receive a printed query letter and self-addressed stamped envelope along with only one sample chapter via Canada Post to begin with, this is exactly what should be submitted. Likewise, if the publishing house wishes to receive the full manuscript and all associated graphics electronically (e.g., via email or the publisher's FTP site), the author should do that. Anyone who ignores these guidelines will surely be denied.

For those wishing to publish through a supportive self-publishing house such as PPG, they will have to submit the entire manuscript and all graphic files altogether in the following manner:

How to Format the Manuscript (Word) File

- Include all front matter, body, back matter, and back cover copy in this document in exactly the order you wish to see it appear in the final designed version of your book (NOTE: back cover copy should be placed at the very end and labelled Back Cover Copy, so the designer knows to move it to the cover, but it must be included in this document so it can be properly edited along with everything else).

- Leave room for the copyright page within your front matter (i.e., simply insert a blank page that says "Insert copyright page here," and PPG will take care of the rest of that page for you).

- Times New Roman or Calibri fonts are fine, 11 pt. size.

- Left-aligned text.

- Double-space the entire document.

- The only hard returns in this document should be at the end of chapter titles and paragraphs.

- Insert a page break at the end of each section and chapter.

- Insert an additional page break where you want a blank page to appear.

- Type [Insert *image file name* here with the following caption: *caption text*] wherever you wish to see your electronic photo files inserted (please refer to the File Prep webpage on PPG's primary website www.polishedpublishinggroup.com for samples of acceptable file names that properly follow PPG's file naming conventions).

- Italicize any words and phrases that you wish to see italicized in the formatted version of your book.

- Bold any words and phrases that you wish to see bolded in the formatted version of your book.

- Underline any words and phrases that you wish to see underlined in the formatted version of your book.

- Capitalize any words and phrases that you wish to see capitalized in the formatted version of your book.

How to Format all Associated Graphic Files

- All colour images should be submitted in either JPEG (.jpg) or TIFF (.tif) format, with a minimum resolution of 300 DPI, using the CMYK (cyan, magenta, yellow, black=key) colour model.

- All black and white images should be submitted in either JPEG (.jpg) or TIFF (.tif) format with a minimum resolution of 300 DPI. For best results, they should be sent as grayscale and monochrome rather than CMYK colour.

- Each file should be associated with the book title and name and should indicate its individual purpose. (Please refer to the File Prep webpage on PPG's primary website www.polishedpublishinggroup.com for samples of acceptable file names that properly follow PPG's file naming conventions.)

- Writers should also include a brief description of their design preferences (including what fonts that they would like used throughout the book).

How to Send Further Important Instructions to the Editor, Proofreader, and Designer

PPG has included an important Production Questionnaire form at the bottom of our Publishing Agreement webpage on PPG's primary website www.polishedpublishinggroup.com. This form must be filled out and submitted at the same time that the interior and cover files are sent because it includes room for additional instructions that the author might wish to relay to the editor or graphic designer.

Additional instructions for the editor and proofreader might be these:

- Please ensure that my manuscript is edited and proofread using PPG's Canadianized style guide that combines the Oxford Style Manual to convert American spellings to the Canadian–British equivalent and the Chicago Manual of Style for punctuation.

Additional instructions for the graphic designer might be these:

- Exclude all headers and footers from the front matter or back matter of this book. Only include them within the body of the book.

- Place only one numerical, centred footer on the first page of each new chapter or section, indicating that page number in place of a header on that page.

- Ensure that all other headers in each section have the title of the book on each left-hand page alternating with the title of the current chapter or section on each right-hand page.

You might want to send ahead of time many other types of instructions to ensure that the book is formatted in the way you want it. Feel free to browse PPG's Production Questionnaire for ideas.

ISBNS AND BARCODES

Any book that is being published to sell for a profit must contain an ISBN and a barcode on its cover. As a matter of fact, every version of that book must have its own ISBN and barcode (i.e., the paperback version will have one, the ebook version will have another one, and the hardcover version will have yet a different one).

Canadian authors must have a Canadian street address to obtain Canadian ISBNs for their books. PPG will apply for all Canadian ISBNs and obtain the associated barcodes on our Canadian authors' behalfs during the design stages of the publishing process. The author–self-publisher will be indicated as both the author and the publisher on that ISBN application so the book is properly linked to the true copyright owner rather than to PPG.

PPG will also aid authors from other countries in publishing and selling their books so long as they supply us with an ISBN from their country for each version of their book that they wish to produce through our company. We will then obtain the associated barcodes for those ISBNs on their behalves.

We automatically produce both POD paperback and Adobe PDF/DRM ebook versions of each book we produce for our authors, so we need two ISBNs to begin with. Some of our authors might also wish to produce a hardcover version in addition to the first two versions, and that's fine. We can do that as long as we also receive a third ISBN for that version of the book along with the others.

What Is an ISBN?

ISBN stands for International Standard Book Number. According to ISBN.org by Bowker (2014),

> The International Standard Book Number (ISBN) is a 13-digit number that uniquely identifies books and book-like products published internationally . . . The purpose of the ISBN is to establish and identify one title or edition of a title from one specific publisher and is unique to that edition, allowing for more efficient marketing of products by booksellers, libraries, universities, wholesalers and distributors.

What Is a Barcode?

According to Data ID Online (2014),

> A bar code can best be described as an 'optical Morse code.' [A series] of black bars and white spaces of varying widths are printed on labels to uniquely identify items.

Barcodes on the back of books hold important information associated with that book such as its recommended retail price when a retailer for sale scans it.

COPYRIGHT PAGE

PPG will insert a pre-designed copyright page into your manuscript for you before it is sent to the designer. All we ask of you is that you leave a blank page in the front matter of your manuscript to accommodate that copyright page and that you make sure to proofread this copyright page to ensure that the ISBNs and all other information are correct.

PUBLISHING AGREEMENTS

PPG will manage all vendor agreements with work-made-for-hire vendors (such as graphic designers, editors, ghostwriters, copywriters, indexers, et cetera) on your behalf. Our agreements are designed to ensure that you receive the high quality service you are paying for in a timely fashion, while maintaining the creative control and copyright ownership of the book and artwork that is being designed for you.

PROFESSIONAL EDITING

The introduction of supported self-publishing has given authors more creative control over their books. They ultimately have the final say, but some fundamentals remain.

The Types of Editing

There are different levels of editing depending on the type of publisher you're dealing with, the type of project you're working on, and the budget you have allotted to the production of your book. For example, traditional literary publishers put each and every fictional novel's manuscript through a very thorough and professional process of substantive editing, stylistic editing, copy editing, *and* proofreading to ensure a polished and saleable result. There are several pairs of eyes on every raw manuscript and galley proof all the way through the process to ensure that 99 percent of every last error is caught and corrected before it goes to print.

A supportive self-publishing house that is producing, for example, a non-fiction "how-to" book will generally stick with copy editing and proofreading to produce the final polished result. In PPG's business model, copy editing and proofreading are mandatory; however, authors who wish to produce the next classic novel are highly encouraged to invest in the full editing process of a traditional literary publisher.

Copy Editing

We will thoroughly review your manuscript in MS Word.doc format and correct any issues with spelling, grammar, and punctuation throughout. We'll also make helpful suggestions regarding word choice and sentence structure, using the English language style of your choice (i.e., Canadian, British, American, et cetera). The edited version will be returned to you for final approval before moving onto the next publishing stage.

Stylistic Editing

Sometimes, you want a little more than a copy edit. A stylistic edit will cover all the points of a copy edit, plus it will eliminate jargon and redundancies, clarify meaning, and ensure that the writing matches the intended audience. Our stylistic edits are completed using the English language style of your choice (i.e., Canadian, British, American, et cetera). The edited version will be returned to you for final approval before moving onto the next publishing stage.

Substantive (Structural) Editing

Do you want the help of a professional editor to improve the overall structure of your manuscript? A substantive edit will cover all the points of a stylistic edit, plus it will clarify and reorganize your entire story for you. These changes are negotiated with you all along the way. Our substantive edits are completed using the English language style of your choice (i.e., Canadian, British, American, et cetera). The edited version will be returned to you for final approval before moving onto the next publishing stage.

Why Even the Best Writers Use Professional Copy Editors

Why do some greenhorn authors resist having their work copy edited by a professional? Perhaps, three underlying reasons are the cause: one, they fear that their work might be stolen if they share it with a stranger prior to publication; two, they fear that the context of their work might be changed during the editing process; and three, they fear the price. Let's address each of these concerns one at a time.

- ### Fear of Copyright Infringement

  First and foremost, the chances of anyone having his or her manuscript stolen and published by someone else—particularly an editor—is next to nil; however, writers can give themselves peace of mind by protecting their copyright ahead of time. Doing so will help to alleviate this fear.

- ### Fear of Changed Context (Loss of Personal Voice)

  It is important to understand that a copy editor's job is simply to enhance a writer's story as it is—to offer helpful suggestions that might have been overlooked or not considered at all.

  Simple copy improvements:

  A second set of eyes will catch those unobvious errors—such as transposed words and letters, punctuation issues, or improper word usage—that an author is simply blind to after reading the same thing over and over again (and that electronic spell checks sometimes miss).

Story development improvements:

Have you ever been trained for a new position by someone who knew the job so well that he or she unconsciously went about many of the details and neglected to discuss them with you? He or she had been doing it for so long themselves that they were unaware of everything they were doing. As a result, you received only part of the information, which made it difficult to follow the entire process from start to finish. In much the same way, writers can sometimes see a scene so vividly in their own minds that, when they transfer it to paper, they unwittingly leave out important details that the reader will need. A good editor will point this out and ask the question, "How exactly did we get from 'A' to 'B' here?" This type of commentary gives writers an opportunity to go back and fill in the blanks that they didn't realize existed beforehand. (This is more common than you might realize!)

Professional copy editors work with writers to enhance their stories while keeping the original voice intact, and the smartest and most successful writers all take that advice seriously. It's important.

- **Fear of the Price of Copy Editing**

There is the *price* of something—and then there is the *cost*. At the very least, a professional copy edit is usually priced at around $0.025 CDN per word, which equates to $750 CDN on a 30,000-word manuscript. This can seem excessive to some new writers who are just breaking into the book publishing business. However, you should consider two important things here: the upfront financial investment that ensures a quality, saleable product (the price); or the loss of sales on the back end that stems from an unprofessional product, riddled with errors (the cost). The best writers know the value of a professional copy edit, and they make sure to have it done on every book they publish. The price is worth it because it will reduce unnecessary costs down the road.

Working With a Copy Editor to Polish a Book

The reality is that self-publishers' books are competing in the marketplace with trade publishers' books. Trade (traditional) publishers always have their books professionally edited. Always. This is why they can boast such high quality. In light of this, a qualified supportive self-publishing house like PPG will require all of its authors to go through a professional copy edit.

Manuscripts must be formatted as indicated earlier on as this clean format makes each paragraph easier for a copy editor to read and correct. The edited manuscript is then returned to the author, via email, in a similar format; however, it will contain highlighted editor's notes that can be read and accepted or declined, one at a time, using MS Word's edit mode (a.k.a. tracking mode or review mode).

The Same Old Emotions

All authors can expect to go through a series of emotions during the copy editing process, both while they are waiting to receive the edited manuscript back and when they view it for the first time. It is the same whether those authors are working with a supportive self-publishing house or a traditional trade publisher. It is natural to feel some initial resistance to an editor's recommendations, and it's common to feel a bit emotional. After all, this isn't a mere book—it is an author's blood, sweat, tears, heart, and soul.

Recognizing this, authors should read the edited manuscript over once, and then put it away for a couple of days to give their emotions time to settle. If they do this, it will be easier to read it over again a second time with a more objective mindset. In that objective state, they can then feel free to go through each change, one by one, and either accept or decline it using MS

Word's edit mode. All authors make better decisions in the objective state, regarding which changes are valid and really should be retained, than they do in that initial emotional state.

The Final Word

Self-publishers are paying all their own production costs to retain 100 percent copyright ownership of their books; therefore, they ultimately have the final word on everything from editing to design to production—as they should! That said, with this level of creative control comes a higher level of responsibility. It is the self-publishers' duty to review and approve their books at every stage along the way. They alone are accountable for the final product; so it is important for self-publishers to go over everything themselves—in addition to the contributions of the editors, indexers, graphic designers, proofreaders, et cetera—before approving anything. This will ensure that they produce a professional final product that can stand proudly beside its competitors.

PROFESSIONAL GRAPHIC DESIGN

The next step in the book publishing process is graphic design. Once you've sent your approved copy edited manuscript back to PPG's project manager, it is then forwarded to one of our professional graphic designers along with all your graphics and the Production Questionnaire instructions.

Professional graphic design is a critical part of the book publishing process, and it is as important to an ebook as it is to a paperback or hardcover. No matter how engaging your story might be, people are going to "judge your book by its cover" before they ever decide to read it. Yet, it won't stop there. They'll not only judge it by the cover design; they'll also judge it by the interior design. Just as not all editors are equal, a noticeable difference is apparent between a book designed by a human or mechanical "template builder" and one designed by a professional graphic artist. As such, the graphic design of your book—both inside and out—should receive the same professional attention as the content itself.

Browse a Bookstore to See What You Like

When deciding how you would like your book's cover and interior to appear, it is best to browse a bookstore (whether in person or online) and view the many different examples there first. What designs, colours, and fonts draw your attention the most? Write down the book titles and author names, so you can use this as a handy reference when it comes time to provide a description to your assigned graphic designer. This will help the process run much more smoothly for both of you.

It is very important to put a lot of thought into the design of your book rather than just leaving it to chance. Graphic designers can only take what is given to them and create the book from there. It's downright dangerous to give someone a simple instruction such as "You choose the font for me" or "You choose the colour for me" because that's exactly what the designer will do—choose it for you depending on his or her own personal preferences. What if that designer didn't fully understand what you were after? What if you end up not liking it at all because of that? As a result, you might end up paying extra for a complete redo down the road. So, it's best to do your homework ahead of time and provide as much detail to the designer as possible by fully answering all the questions on PPG's online Production Questionnaire.

Your Book Title Is Important

This book has a long name, doesn't it? So did the book I wrote last year . . . and with good reason. A book title must be concise enough to appeal to readers *visually*—to let them know what it's about in one quick glance. In this day and age, with so many books now selling online, the title should also take advantage of the power of keywords in online searches (whenever possible) as discussed in the marketing section of this book.

You saw, earlier on, the value of incorporating one of my major keywords "how to publish a book in Canada" into last year's book and how that improved my book's standing on a major search engine without me even personally paying for that pay-per-click ad. (To this day, I don't know who paid for it! But it was online for over a week! That's worth a lot of money!) I'm using the same online marketing technique with this book by incorporating two more of my company's major key words into the title: "how to publish a bestselling book" and "sell based on value, not price."

How do you know what your major keywords are? Play around on Google and Yahoo, two of the top search engines. Type in the words you think people might be typing when they're searching for your particular topic. Adjust the title of your book accordingly.

Here are the two tests I did to determine the title of my new book:

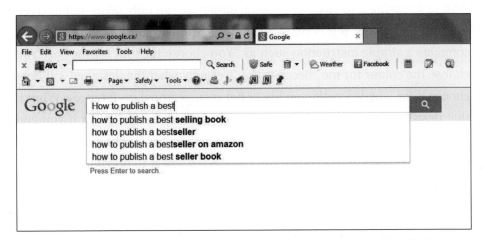

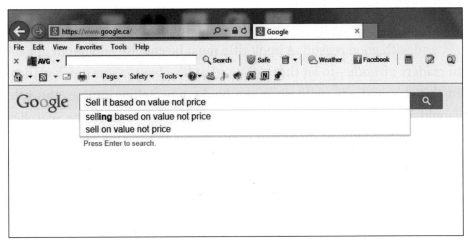

Interior Design

PPG will begin by designing your book's interior because the spine size of your book cover is determined by the final page count of your book; and the final page count of your book can only be determined once the interior design is complete. A book's interior is comprised of three basic elements: front matter, the body, and back matter. Each element might differ slightly depending on the type of book being published. For example, a non-fiction book will contain an index in its back matter whereas a fictional novel will not. Following is a list to provide you with some inspiration for your own book.

The front matter of a book might contain some or all of the following components:

- Primary title page: This is usually the very first page of the book in which the title appears on an otherwise blank right-hand page.

- Secondary title page: The secondary title page repeats the book title along with the author and publisher's name on the next right-hand page.

- Copyright page: Typically, the publishing company will insert the copyright page into the book's front matter on behalf of the author–self-publisher. In anticipation of this, the author–self-publisher should leave room in the front matter of their manuscript to accommodate it. The copyright page will contain the book's ISBN(s), publication date, copyright owner's name, and a copyright notice such as, "No portion of this book may be duplicated or used in any form by any electronic or mechanical means (including photocopying, recording, or information storage and retrieval) for any profit- driven enterprise without prior permission in writing from the publisher." If the author also wishes to credit any of the book's contributors (e.g., photographers and designers), that can also be done on this page.

- Quote page: Sometimes a quote will be placed in the front matter if it sums up the essence of the story quite well.

- Dedication page: Oftentimes, authors will dedicate their books to their loved ones. That dedication is placed in the beginning of the book.

- Acknowledgments page: An acknowledgments page allows an author to provide more detail when crediting the book's various contributors rather than just listing their names on the copyright page. Here, a heartfelt thank you can be expressed in a much more meaningful way.

- Foreword: Usually, a foreword is written by someone other than the author. Its purpose is to provide a history leading up to the story being told or explain what inspired the publication of the book.

- Preface: Where a foreword is an introduction to the book written by someone other than the author, a preface is an introduction written by the author for the same purpose. An author might also use a preface to explain what methods of research were used during the creation of the work.

- Contents: A table of contents lists the various sections (i.e., chapters, articles, poems, et cetera) within the book and that page numbers on which they begin.

The body of a book usually contains at least the following two components:

- Title Pages: A title page is used at the beginning of each section within the body of a book. The purpose of the title page is simply to differentiate between the sections to help organize the flow of the work.

- Sections: Sections of a book's body can be divided up as chapters, poems, articles, et cetera. It all depends on the type of book being published.

The back matter of a book might contain some or all of the following components:

- Appendix: An appendix contains supplementary details that help to clarify further any legal, technical, or scientific information within the book.

- Bibliography: A bibliography is a list of the books, articles, webpages, et cetera, that were sourced and referred to throughout the book.

- Glossary: A glossary of terms contains a list of specialized words that can be found throughout the book along with their definitions.

- Index: An alphabetized index is used to help readers pinpoint the exact pages where they can find an important name, place, or subject throughout the book. (All non-fiction books produced by PPG are required to have an index.)

- Promotional Content: A great way to sell your back list titles is to promote them in the back matter of each new release. It is best if you can provide a graphic of each book's front cover along with the corresponding ISBNs. This way, readers can search for these back list titles online or at bookstores if they wish to purchase them.

- Author Biography: An updated author biography helps personalize your book for readers by giving them a bit more information about the storyteller. It is also a great way to promote past titles, thereby increasing the chance of more sales.

Take a moment to browse the various elements of the POD paperback version of *this* non-fiction book for inspiration. It's not only a great example of how you might format your own front matter, body, and back matter; but it also provides a professional header and footer sample for those who are unsure of what to do in this area.

Cover Design

There are many different types of book covers ranging from case laminate or dust jacketed hard covers to perfect bound paperbacks to ebooks. Although they each have their own unique requirements in content and design, some basic components are common to most books. Using this author's own paperback books as examples, you can see that a complete book cover is made up of at least the following three components: the back cover, the spine, and the front cover.

Back Cover

As shown in the upcoming visual aid, the back cover portion of your complete book cover begins on the left-hand side. The dimension of the back cover must match whatever trim size you've chosen your book to be (i.e., 5.5 x 8.5 inches as shown in the examples) with a minimum 1/4-inch bleed around the outside edges for trimming. It will also contain the following features:

- An author photo (optional)
- Back cover copy (marketing copy that summarizes the contents of the book in a compelling way)
- Room for the book's barcode and ISBN on the lower right-hand corner
- Room for PPG's logo on the lower left-hand corner
- A short author biography (optional)

Spine

The spine portion of your complete book cover sits in between your back and front cover. Its height will match your chosen trim size (in the case of these examples 8.5 inches), while the width is determined by factors such as the final page count of your designed interior and chosen weight of paper. The spine also contains the following features:

- The book title at the top
- Author name (pseudonym) in the centre
- Room for PPG's logo to be placed at the bottom

Front Cover

The front cover portion of your complete book cover sits on the right-hand side. The dimension of the front cover must match whatever trim size you've chosen your book to be (i.e., 5.5 x 8.5 inches as shown in the examples) with a minimum 1/4-inch bleed around the outside edges for trimming. It will also contain the following features:

- The book title (and subtitle, if applicable)
- Author name (pseudonym)

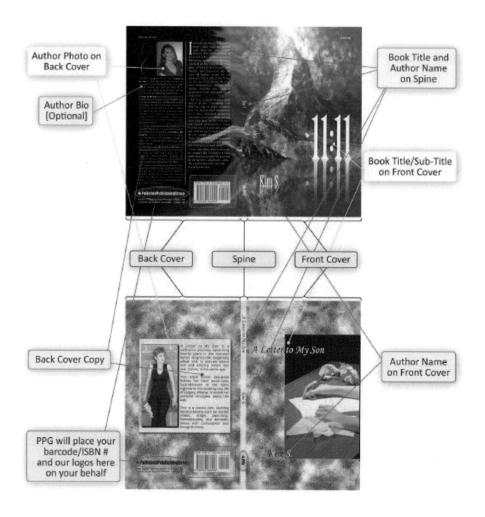

Author Photos

Author photos make as powerful a statement about a writer as a book cover makes about the story inside. As such, this photo should be given as much care and consideration as the rest of the book. When it comes to author photos, "attractive" can come in all kinds of forms.

The back cover of a book is a great place to put an author photo, but sometimes it's just as well to put it on the front. It can be a simple headshot or full-length portrait, depending on the writer's preference; and this is a great place to get creative. A professional photographer knows how to use either colour or black and white to depict the mood of the story within the author photo. To make the picture even more attractive to readers, writers can dress themselves up as a character from inside their books or create the setting of the book within the background of the picture.

Artwork

Your cover artwork can wrap around the spine of your book and span the entire height and width of the complete cover (as shown in the first visual for the book titled *11:11,* 978-0-9864869-4-4 on Amazon); it can appear on the front cover only (as shown in the second visual for the book titled *A Letter to My Son,* 978-0-9864869-0-6 on Amazon); or it can be more complex (as shown in the third visual, on the following page, for the book titled *A Letter to My Daughter,* 978-0-9864869-2-0 on Amazon).

All of these examples are correct. If going with the first example, make sure the artwork itself contains a minimum 1/4-inch bleed all around the edges, so the outside edges of the picture aren't trimmed unnecessarily at the printer. If going with the third example, keep in mind that additional graphics require additional work for the designer, which will equate to additional upfront costs for the self-publishing author.

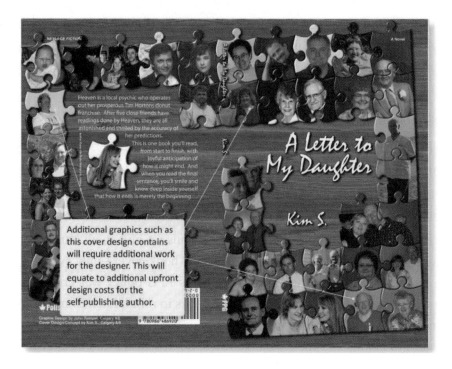

NEW/AGE FICTION

A Novel

Heaven is a local psychic who operates out her prosperous Tim Hortons donut franchise. After five close friends have readings done by Heaven, they are all astonished and thrilled by the accuracy of her predictions.

This is one book you'll read, from start to finish, with joyful anticipation of how it might end. And when you read the final sentence, you'll smile and know deep inside yourself that how it ends is merely the beginning...

A Letter to My Daughter

Kim S.

Additional graphics such as this cover design contains will require additional work for the designer. This will equate to additional upfront design costs for the self-publishing author.

Graphic Design by John Temple, Calgary AB
Cover Design Concept by Kim S., Calgary AB

9 780986 486920

Author Proofing Rounds

The graphic design portion of PPG's book publishing process includes the following features:

- Two sample cover designs and two sample interior designs (emailed to the self-publishing author in .PDF format) from which that author can choose his or her favourite one of each to use in the creation of the book

- A half hour phone consultation with the graphic designer, if required (or an in-person coffee shop meeting if both are located in the same city)

- Two electronic (.PDF) proofing rounds during which the author can make up to five basic structural changes to the cover and up to 50 minor typographical changes to the interior per round if needed

At this stage in the game, very few changes should need to be made. These two proofing rounds really should be sufficient; however, any authors who require more than the standard two proofing rounds can feel free to purchase them as add-ons to their packages.

PPG's Graphic Design Style Guide

Just as PPG has created an editorial style guide to ensure consistency and continuity from each one of our professional editors, we've also created a graphic design style guide to ensure the same from each of our professional designers.

An example of one of the standard instructions we give to all our designers is to never include a visual of price on a PPG book cover—only ever include the barcode, excluding the visual price. This PPG policy was created with the worldwide online distribution of our books in mind. Each country has its own currency, and the prices of books outside North America might fluctuate because of changes in the exchange rates. So, it's easier and cleaner to just leave the price off altogether.

PPG provides many more instructions to our designers, and our style guides are always being improved along the way with input from the vendors involved. By doing so, PPG's authors can be assured the same superior quality from every one of our vendors on every one of their books.

FACT CHECKING AND INDEXING

Non-fiction readers expect to find an index in the back of your book. They also expect your information to be completely accurate. You can hire fact checkers and indexers through PPG to help you accomplish this.

So, what exactly is an index, and why would anyone look for one at the back of your book if that book already has a table of contents at the beginning? Tia Leschke (2010) explained it perfectly with this comment, "A good index is a roadmap to information. It leads readers to all the information on a particular subject, and it also leads readers to related information that might interest them."

Where a non-fiction book's table of contents can direct readers to whole sections of a book where they might find a particular topic of interest, an alphabetized index takes it a step further by allowing readers to pinpoint the exact pages within the book where specific names or terms can be located. For example, an author might want to refer back to a specific detail in this book that discusses POD technology, but he or she may not recall exactly which page that detail was on. The quickest way to find it is by referring to the index at the back of this book where all the possible pages are indicated together in one place beside that term.

Indexes can be as helpful in ebooks as they are in paperbacks and hardcovers. PPG automatically produces an Adobe PDF/DRM ebook along with the POD paperback version of the book; therefore, they are formatted consistently with the index intact. We also employ a professional ebook conversion service whose staff know how to adjust that index within the new file format to ensure that it remains intact.

The indexing portion of PPG's book publishing process is completed immediately after the self-publishing author has approved the final interior design of the book in .PDF format. From there, the approved .PDF is sent to the indexer to complete the index in MS Word format based on this final word placement, and that MS Word.doc is then returned to the designer to pop into the back matter of the book. From here, the first hard copy (physical proof) of the book is printed and sent to one of PPG's professional proofreaders for yet another once over with yet another fresh set of eyes.

PROFESSIONAL PROOFREADING

Where a copy editor's job is to review and improve an author's raw manuscript, and the graphic designer's job is to arrange that raw edited text into a professional and appealing layout, a professional proofreader provides yet another set of eyes to ensure that all the components fit together properly and the book is ready for public viewing and printing. The proofreader's job is to complete the following nine-point check:

Interior Check

- The front matter (such as the table of contents) is accurate and correct.
- The back matter (such as the index) is accurate and correct.
- Headers and footers are accurate and correct.
- Bad breaks, widows, and orphans are eliminated.
- Text is kerned to flow smoothly throughout.
- Margins and trim size all measure properly.
- Spelling and punctuation is correct.

Cover Check

- Spacing, bleeds, and trim size all measure properly.
- Spelling and punctuation is correct.

As shown in the above list, a professional proofreader is someone who is knowledgeable and experienced with both basic language editing (spelling and punctuation) as well as the technical aspects of book design (kerning, bleeds, trim size, et cetera). If the proofreader finds any issues in the layout, he or she will indicate these and send them back to the designer to make the corrections. Once these corrections are completed, a second hard copy (physical proof) of the book is printed and sent to the self-publishing author for one last overview before the final approval and sign-off of the book.

The Final Word

All of PPG's professional editors, designers, and proofreaders will do their part to help polish and perfect every PPG book all along the way, but it is worth repeating again that the self-publisher is ultimately responsible to ensure his or her book is completely correct before signing off on the final hard-copy proof. It is recommended (and wise) to re-read everything over one more time before signing a final proof approval—not only the recent corrections, but everything—even after the professional proofread has been completed. It takes some extra time to do this, but it is well worth it in the end.

More Emotions

Once again, self-publishing authors can expect to go through a series of emotions during the final proofreading portion of the book publishing process. At this stage, they might find themselves feeling a bit anxious about upcoming printing costs and public book signings, and they might be impatient with how long everything seems to be taking. The only words of relief I can give are this: it's the nature of the beast, it's all perfectly natural, it's okay, and it will all be well worth it when you hold that final, finished product in your hands for the first time.

How To Price A Paperback Book: Setting Your Retail Price

When you're trying to figure out your initial publishing costs, you need to know how many words and graphics will be in the interior, will it be a colour or black and white interior, and what trim size will the book be created as. Figuring out your printing costs is a bit different. It is only once the book is fully formatted and we know all the above information plus the final page count of the formatted book (including all back matter such as the index) that we can request a printing quote.

We've already touched on the importance of having a well thought-out sales and marketing plan that takes your target market into consideration when setting the retail price of your book. That said, two more important things must be considered when it comes time to sit down to decide at what retail price you will set your paperback book: who will print it and who will sell it. These decisions must be made because different types of printers are available to use, depending on how many books you want to print, and because the various booksellers (retail and wholesale) will take different percentage cuts of your retail price for their profits. So, it is important to take all of these things into consideration—including how much profit you intend to earn from your book sales—*before* you decide on your recommended retail price.

Who's Printing Your Book for You?

There are three primary types of printers that are most competitively priced in three different types of situations: POD printers are typically best for printing one to 99 copies; digital printers are typically best for 100–999 copies; and offset printers are typically best for 1,000+ copies. Here is a generic graphic to illustrate how much a 6 x 9-inch paperback with a 180-page black and white interior might cost to print (these prices are NOT set in stone—this is just a sample to illustrate a point):

Sample Printing Prices (Per Unit) for 6" X 9" Paperback Book with 180-Page Black and White Interior							
Print-on-Demand (POD) 1-99 copies Paperback Only	Digital - 100 Paperback	Digital - 250 Paperback	Digital - 500 Paperback	Offset - 1,000 Paperback	Offset - 2,000 Paperback	Offset - 2,500 Paperback
$4.50	$4.45	$4.30	$4.23	$2.64	$1.74	$1.58

Obviously, the upside to printing higher quantities of your books (1,000+) with an offset printer is that you will enjoy the lowest cost per unit which will also translate into the highest profit per unit overall. The downside to printing this many books is the higher upfront cost (i.e., $2,640 + tax and shipping on 1,000 books at a cost of $2.64 per book). It also means that you'll have to keep thousands of books stored away in a warehouse and then work hard to sell them all off. Authors are only encouraged to print 1,000+ books if they truly believe that they will be able to sell 1,000+ books—if they have a well thought-out sales and marketing plan in place.

For some people, the idea of coming up with an additional $2,640 + tax and shipping is too much—especially after they've just spent $2,500+ on the publishing costs associated with their books. For other people, they simply have no idea how they will be able to sell that many books, anyway. For these authors, it makes more sense to start small and print lower quantities of their books at a digital printer. Alternatively, in some cases, it might even make better sense *not* to print any at all, but merely to sell their books through Amazon on a POD basis.

Many people are surprised to learn that ecommerce booksellers like Amazon don't actually keep any physical books in stock anywhere. They simply keep a copy of the digital files for each book in their digital database; and they will print, bind, and ship them one at a time "on demand" as customers buy them—hence the term print-on-demand (POD). This technology is amazing! What's most amazing about it is that it alleviates the need for self-publishing authors to print large quantities of their books that they might or might not be able to sell.

The digital files for all of PPG's paperback books are automatically uploaded to Amazon for them. The digital files for all of PPG's ebooks are automatically uploaded to sites such as KoboBooks.com and eBookMall.com for them. These sites are where PPG tries to sell extra copies of our authors' books for them and for our own profit. They are also where authors can feel free to direct customers to buy their books in the event they choose not to print any of them at all.

PPG gives its authors back all of their working files and finished digital files once the final proof of their books have been approved so that they can shop around for the best possible printers depending on their individual needs (i.e., best service, best price). We will get the first printing quote for you and explain how and why it all works the way it does; after that, you've got your files and you can do as you please on your own.

Of course, as per PPG's publishing agreement (PPG, 2013), it is understood that the company is also trying to earn a wee bit of a profit from the sale of our authors' books for any of the POD books that are sold on sites such as Amazon and PPG's online store on your behalf. For these sales, an author–self-publisher's profit will be indirect in the form of royalties we'll pay to him or her.

By contrast, as with all book publishing business models, any of the wholesale author copies that authors buy and print to sell directly on their own—whether they are printed through PPG's POD partner (one to 99 copies), or through the digital printer of the author's choice (100-999 copies), or through the offset printer of the author's choice (1000+ copies)—the profit will be direct. As such, zero royalties are paid by PPG on these books.

Who's Selling Your Book for You?

Authors always make the most profit on any of the books they sell directly by themselves (i.e., books sold at the back of a room during a speaking tour, books sold at a table at a farmers' market, et cetera) because no middleman is involved in the process. You're just printing them and then selling them, so printing is the only real cost.

That said, if you want help from other people to sell your books on your behalf (which most authors do), you have more to consider before setting the retail price of your book. You'll have to factor in their cut of the profits, and here are the industry standards in terms of the discount requirements of most traditional wholesalers/distributors and retailers:

- Book wholesalers/distributors (i.e., Ingram, Baker & Taylor): usually a 55 percent discount
- Book retailers (i.e., Chapters, Books-A-Million): usually a 40–50 percent discount

If you have a friend or neighbour helping to sell your books for you (at a craft table, for example), you really should give them a cut of those profits as a thank you and payment for their time. Hopefully, they'll be a little cheaper than a traditional bookseller and only cost you 25–35 percent off the retail price of the book.

All that said, whenever authors are trying to figure out at what price they should set their book, I always recommend that they factor in the highest possible printing price (usually it's the POD price) and the highest possible discount (wholesaler/distributor discount) to determine what their lowest possible recommended retail price should be. That's the starting point:

Sample Pricing Spreadsheet (Paperbacks)	
If you set your list price at:	$11.99
less (for example) the POD price/unit:	$4.50
your leftover before any discounts will be:	$7.49
less the highest possible wholesale discount of 55%:	$6.59
your net profit/unit (worst-case scenario) would be:	$0.90

Using the above numbers, the absolute lowest recommended retail price of this sample book—for the author who plans to sell it through both traditional and ecommerce booksellers—should be $11.99. From here, now one can play with the numbers. If a $0.90 lowest possible profit is too low, then set the retail price higher and higher until that bottom number feels comfortable. Just make sure that retail price remains consistent with your overall sales and marketing image (either the best quality or the best price). It's as simple as that.

At the end of the day, that retail price is the author's decision. Whatever PPG's authors tell us that price should be is the price we will indicate to all our booksellers as the recommended retail price. On that note, however, PPG doesn't (nor does any other publisher) determine the individual practices of wholesalers and retailers. Each wholesaler and retailer reserves the right to set its own discounts for the products and services it offers. For example, if it wants to put your book on sale and offer a 35 percent discount off your retail price, it reserves the right to do so.

PPG's policy is to refrain from printing the suggested retail price on any of our book covers for the following reasons: to allow authors the flexibility to offer different pricing at different events; so that books being sold in another country can display the pricing in that country's currency; and because wholesalers and retailers reserve the right to set their own discounts for the products and services they offer.

How Many Copies Do I Have To Sell To Make A Profit?

By this stage in the process, you should have everything you need to finalize the financial aspect of your marketing strategy: you now know your target market; you know the cost of publishing your book; you know the cost of printing your book; and you know the retail price of your book. Here are three sample calculations you can use to determine how many copies you'll have to sell to earn a profit, based on the earlier example retail price of $11.99 per book:

1. If you've determined that your target market is more likely to buy your book online than in traditional bookstores, you might choose not to print any books at all and just sell POD paperback copies and ebooks through sites like Amazon, KoboBooks.com, and eBookMall.com. In this case, your only upfront cost is publishing at $2,500. All other costs will be deducted as the books sell:

Sample Pricing Spreadsheet (Paperbacks)	
If you set your list price at:	$11.99
less (for example) the POD price/unit:	$4.50
your leftover before any discounts will be:	$7.49
less the highest possible wholesale discount of 55%:	$6.59
your net profit/unit (worst-case scenario) would be:	$0.90

Using an expected profit of roughly $0.90 per book, you would have to find a way to sell 2,800 books online just to break even. You would start to see a profit on every book you sold over and above that amount.

2. If you've determined that your target market is more likely to buy your book from a traditional bookstore in your area, and that bookstore has agreed to carry consignment copies of your book and sell them for you for a 45 percent cut, your calculation will be a little different. For example, you might have an upfront publishing cost of $2,500 plus an upfront printing cost of $3,480 for a total of $5,980 in upfront costs to try to recoup in sales.

Sample Pricing Spreadsheet (Paperbacks)	
If you set your list price at:	$11.99
less the Offset 2,000 price/unit:	$1.74
your leftover before any discounts will be:	$10.25
less the retailer's discount of 45%:	$5.40
your net profit/unit (worst-case scenario) would be:	$4.85

On the plus side, with this model, your profit per book has increased dramatically which means you'll only have to sell roughly 1,240 books through that bookseller to break even. You'll start to see a profit on every book you sell up and above that.

3.   If you've determined that your target market is more likely to buy your books directly from you (whether you're selling them at some kind of market, or perhaps at a table at the back of a room where you're speaking to a group of people, or wherever else), your calculation will change again. For example, you might have an upfront publishing cost of $2,500 plus an upfront printing cost of $3,950 for a total of $6,450 in upfront costs to try to recoup in sales.

Sample Pricing Spreadsheet (Paperbacks)	
If you set your list price at:	$11.99
less the Offset 2,500 price/unit:	$1.58
your leftover before any discounts will be:	$10.41
No middleman. Selling direct:	$0.00
your net profit/unit (worst-case scenario) would be:	$10.41

With no middleman, look at how much your profit per unit has increased! Now it will only take the sale of 620 books to break even. The remaining 1,850 books will generate pure profit for you—over $19,000 in pure profit!

Using these three examples, you can begin to see the importance of really thinking through your target market and retail price ahead of time—of learning the skill of selling based on value rather than simply charging the lowest price. You can also see how much more money you can earn in certain situations compared with others. Again, you have to sell your book where your target market is buying. If they're buying online, that's where you need to sell regardless of whether you're going to share that profit with a few middlemen here and there. In cases where you must consider middlemen, it might be wise to increase your retail price by a couple of dollars. Food for thought.

COMPLIMENTARY AND PROMOTIONAL COPIES

It is customary for the publisher (in this case the self-publisher) to send out one complimentary copy of its book to each vendor who helped them to publish it (i.e., the copy editor, designer, indexer, proofreader, photographer, illustrator, et cetera) as a special thank you. It is also common for publishers to send promotional copies to other individuals and organizations who agree to promote the book on their behalf (i.e., publicists).

UNPAID TRADITIONAL BOOK REVIEWS

Another custom among trade publishers that really should be adopted by self-publishing authors is making sure to send out a few complimentary copies of your book to various traditional book reviewers in your area. The upside is that these reviews are free of charge in the sense that your only cost is the copy of your book and the postage to send it; however, the downside is that you're not guaranteed a review after sending it. It's at the discretion of the reviewer.

Two types of unpaid traditional book reviews are available: one, the review that you send out ahead of time, known as an advance reader copy, to stir up interest in the book *before* publication; and two, a published review copy of the actual final edited version of your book.

Advance Reader Copies (Uncorrected Proofs)

These review copies can be printed and mailed out as hard copy galleys or emailed as .PDF files. It is important to ensure they are stamped with the words "Advance Reader Copy (Uncorrected Proof)" on the front cover, and possibly also on every few pages of the interior, to ensure that the reviewer understands the copy is unedited so he or she takes that into account.

Published Review Copies

When sending a final published review copy to an editor, whether mailed as a hard copy or emailed as a .PDF, make sure to stamp "Review Copy" on the front cover of the book so it cannot be resold for profit. This also ensures that it will get to the right person at the newspaper or magazine to which you're sending it for review.

Rachaelle Lynn (2009) provided valuable advice to authors in a blog entry she wrote for PPG about the importance of review copies a few years back:

> Set aside time for making a list of who should receive review copies of your book. Consider the market for it carefully; depending on the genre and subject matter, you may want to submit it to reviewers in smaller, more specialized markets instead of to those at larger publications, where your book could get lost in the crowd. If you'll be visiting particular areas for readings and book signings, locate reviewers in those markets so you'll have advance publicity.

A great book review can help to boost your sales. It's definitely worth the cost of a complimentary book or two.

LIBRARY COPIES

As a self-publisher, it is up to you to produce and submit a flyer or small catalogue of your book(s) to all the libraries you wish to appear in. The only way many libraries learn about new titles is through the flyers and catalogues that they receive from publishers. In Canada, they might also learn about new titles via the copies submitted to Legal Deposit at Library and Archives Canada (LAC) by self-publishers upon publication (as discussed in more detail in *How to Publish a Book in Canada . . . and Sell Enough Copies to Make a Profit!*).

WORLDWIDE DISTRIBUTION

PPG ensures its authors' books are available for sale all around the world for at least two years—longer than that for those who agree to extend their distribution terms with us once the first two years are up. Whether consumers prefer to order PPG books through their favourite bookstores or buy them online, here are merely a few of the many places where they can be found:

North American Distribution Channels

- Amazon
- Baker & Taylor
- Barnes & Noble
- Ingram
- NACSCORP

United Kingdom Distribution Channels

- Adlibris
- Amazon
- Aphrohead
- Bertrams
- Blackwell
- Book Depository
- Coutts
- Eden Interactive, Ltd.
- Gardners
- Mallory International
- Paperback Shop

Online Purchases of PPG Paperback Books

- shop.polishedpublishinggroup.com
- www.amazon.ca
- www.amazon.com
- www.amazon.co.uk
- www.amazon.de
- www.amazon.fr
- www.amazon.es
- www.amazon.it

Online Purchases of PPG eBooks

- www.kobobooks.com
- www.ebookmall.com
- www.AllRomance.com, www.OmniLit.com
- www.artechhouse.com
- www.asiabooks.com
- www.betterworldbooks.com
- www.bilbary.com
- www.bol.com
- www.booktopia.com.au
- www.campusebookstore.com
- www.christiansupply.com/shop/ebooks
- www.completebook.com
- www.deastore.it
- www.ebookmall.com
- www.ebookpie.com
- www.ebookshop.co.za
- www.eCampus.com
- www.emviem.com
- www.feedbooks.com
- www.fishpond.com.au, www.fishpond.co.nz
- www.gohastings.com
- www.infibeam.com
- www.kalahari.net
- www.kobobooks.com
- www.kriso.ee
- www.lailai.com.tw
- www.libri.de
- www.livrariasaraiva.com.br
- www.lybrary.com

- www.mardel.com
- www.mediander.com
- www.mobi-book.com
- www.mphonline.com.my
- www.offworldbooks.com
- www.Paddle.com
- www.parable.com
- www.printsindia.in/
- www.qbend.com
- www.ReadBooks.com
- www.reproindialtd.com
- www.riidr.com
- www.sbs.com.br
- www.shop.ca
- www.suomalainen.com
- www.textbook.com
- www.thecopia.com
- www.tookbook.com
- www.tradebit.com
- www.treefreemobile.com
- www.txtr.com
- www.ubreader.com; www.mobisystems.com
- www.wavecloud.com
- www.webster.it

PPG's self-publishing authors are the copyright owners of their books and retain all of their finished files at the end of the publishing process; therefore, they reserve the right to expand this distribution and sales network even further if they wish. The sky is the limit when you are the owner of your book. Where and how you sell it is up to you—anywhere in the world.

ROYALTIES

PPG authors are paid royalties (in CDN currency) on any of their books we can sell on their behalf through the PPG online bookstore and the various distribution channels mentioned earlier. Royalties are never paid on the wholesale author copies that authors have printed to sell on their own. Although PPG pays a very handsome royalty rate compared to trade industry standards (up to 40 percent, calculated as a percentage of the title's sale price), authors can still expect to earn much more money on the books that they sell on their own (Polished Publishing Group, 2013c).

SECTION FIVE:

{
# Modern Book Printing
# and *Non*-Printing Options
}

"*Creativity* is thinking up new things. *Innovation* is doing new things."

~Theodore Levitt

AN ELEMENTARY INTRODUCTION TO PRINTING

It used to be that, whenever a book was published, there was automatically a large run of 1,000 or more copies of it printed and stored away in a large warehouse by the publisher and/or its distributor(s). This large run meant a higher upfront cost for that publisher on all of its books without any guarantee that they would be able to sell them all off.

Times have changed. Today's self-publishing authors have many more choices available to them. If they want to print that many books straight away, they still can. Alternatively, they can choose to print fewer numbers of books at a time (i.e., 250 copies) as selling opportunities arise. Alternatively yet, they can even choose to *not* print any physical copies of their books at all, but simply to sell digital versions of them online. The sky is the limit nowadays, and this is good news for self-publishers.

Below is an elementary introduction to the various printing (and non-printing) options available to today's authors. For those who wish to delve deeper into any one of these options, the best thing to do is to contact that type of printer directly. Better yet, go take a tour of their facility to gain a much better understanding of their machinery and processes.

EBOOKS

Not long ago, the only option available to environmentally conscious book buyers was to check the inside of a paperback to ensure that it was printed on FSC-certified paper. Now another option is available that doesn't require any paper at all: ebooks. This is good news for consumers and publishers alike.

Ebooks are electronic, so they are the digital equivalent to conventional printed books and can be downloaded directly to a computer or hand-held ebook reading device (i.e., e-reader) in a matter of minutes. This technology enables consumers to purchase books from the comfort of their homes and offices without worrying about wasted paper or shipping and handling fees. It allows people to store several books in one keyword-searchable, lightweight container. Plus, it saves publishers (particularly self-publishers) from paying the upfront expenses associated with printing, storage, distribution, and book returns. The benefits of this new technology are numerous!

There are several ebook file formats to choose from; and there are even more software programs and hardware devices designed to download and view them. To keep things simple, PPG automatically produces an Adobe PDF/DRM ebook version of all its authors' POD paperback books and sells them online through ecommerce sites such as KoboBooks.com and eBookMall.com. (DRM stands for Digital Rights Management, which protects the copyright of the PDF ebook by preventing people from copying, printing, emailing, or sharing it with others free of charge.) For our authors who want their ebooks available in even more online markets than we already offer, our ebook file conversion service can convert their Adobe PDF/DRM ebook file into any number of different file formats, including EPUB 2, EPUB 3, Mobi, AZW, KF8, Epub and Kindle Fixed, making the book available on several different devices, including Kindle Fire, Kindle, Nook, Kobo, iPad, iTouch, iPhone, Android devices, Sony Reader, Adobe Digital Editions, and Mobipocket. Authors can then upload the additional files to the ebook ecommerce sites of their choice to use as additional distributors of their book.

Print-On-Demand (POD)

Wikipedia (2013d) provided a great description of what POD technology is:

> Print on demand (POD) is a printing technology and business process in which new copies of a book (or other document) are not printed until an order has been received, which means books can be printed one at a time. While 'build to order' has been an established business model in many other industries, 'print on demand' developed only after digital printing began . . . because it was not economical to print single copies using traditional printing technology such as letterpress and offset printing.

PPG automatically submits a copy of the digital files of every PPG authors' paperback books to the Amazon group of ecommerce sites around the world. Amazon uses POD technology to sell books online. The biggest benefit to this is that it provides PPG's authors with worldwide online distribution of the paperback versions of their books without any upfront printing costs whatsoever.

When digitally signing a PPG publishing agreement, self-publishing authors are agreeing to this worldwide POD distribution (as well as the earlier-mentioned ebook distribution) of their titles for a period of two years. At the end of those two years, they can opt out of this distribution channel or pay a small fee to continue it for another term. This option is another way PPG tries to be as flexible with our authors as possible. At the end of the day, most authors would agree that online POD distribution is highly valuable and opt to continue on with it indefinitely.

DIGITAL PRINTING

Regarding digital printing,

> Digital printing refers to methods of printing from a digital image directly to a variety of media . . . . It usually refers to professional printing where small-run jobs from desktop publishing and other digital sources are printed using large-format and high-volume laser or inkjet printers. Digital printing has a higher cost per page than more traditional offset printing methods, but this price is usually offset by avoiding the cost of all the technical steps required to make printing plates. (Wikipedia, 2013a)

Digital printers are very similar to POD printers in that they both use digital files (camera-ready .PDFs) of a book's interior and cover to produce the physical version of the book. The differentiator is simply in the technology— the fact is that a POD printer can easily and economically produce one copy of a book at a time, whereas a digital printer can usually only be competitive at printing a minimum of 100 copies of a book.

OFFSET PRINTING

Last but not least is offset printing—the traditional printing method whereby 1000+ copies of a book can be printed at an economical price.

> Offset lithography is one of the most common ways of creating printed matter. A few of its common applications include newspapers, magazines, brochures, stationery, and books. Compared to other printing methods, offset printing is best suited for economically producing large volumes of high quality prints in a manner that requires little maintenance . . . . Many modern offset presses use computer to plate systems as opposed to the older computer to film work flows, which further increases their quality. (Wikipedia, 2013c)

As discussed all through this book, there is a time and a place for each of these printing and non-printing options. At the end of the day, it all depends on to whom a book will be sold, how many copies will be sold, where those copies will be sold, and how much of a profit the self-publishing author wishes to make. POD printers are typically best for printing one to 99 copies, digital printers are typically best for printing 100-999 copies, and offset printers are typically best for printing 1,000+ copies. Then again, an author might want to sell only digital ebook versions of their books and not print anything at all. There's beauty in this, isn't there? Choice is a very good thing.

SECTION SIX:

{ # Final Words of Advice }

"Whatever you do, do it well. Do it so well that when people see you do it they will want to come back and see you do it again and they will want to bring others and show them how well you do what you do."

~Walt Disney

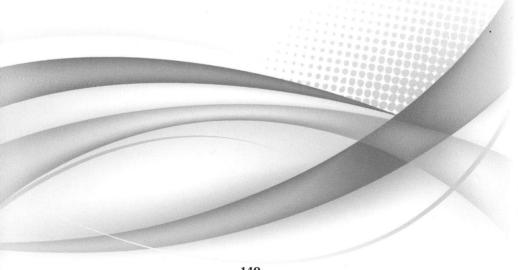

AUTHORS ARE ENTREPRENEURS

To be a truly successful author that can sell enough books to earn a profit and possibly even become a bestseller, you must treat book publishing, sales, and marketing as your own business. The same holds true whether you take today's supported self-publishing route or you go with a traditional trade publisher. If you enter into this venture with the expectation that you won't have to invest much of your own time or money—or that your publisher is solely responsible for these investments on your behalf—you'll most likely be disappointed by how few books you sell. However, if you go into this with an entrepreneurial spirit, you might just find your wings.

You move books by getting in front of your customers and communicating with them in a clear and consistent manner; and you do this by virtue of book signings, readings, craft sales, art shows, media tours, social media campaigns, speaking engagements, book reviews, and whatever else you can think of whenever and wherever you can. You "pound the pavement," as we say in the sales world. You do the work that's necessary to make yourself stand out among all the rest for your particular genre.

PPG has built up a fantastic team of professional editors, designers, proofreaders, indexers, ghostwriters, and publicists (i.e., bloggers, social media experts, et cetera) that can help you manage all (or portions) of your book's publishing, sales, and marketing if you prefer to invest more money than time. We've also created the PPG Publisher's Blog and PPG Writers Forum, and we've filled both with all kinds of helpful information for the authors who are more comfortable spending more of their time than their money. We recognize that everyone has unique requirements in this regard, and we're here to help. We strive to make things as easy for PPG's entrepreneurial authors as possible by educating them and arming them with the tools they'll need to be successful.

On that note, here are a few final words of advice to help you along your journey to success.

YOUR BOOK WILL NEVER BE GOOD ENOUGH FOR YOU: LEARNING WHEN TO LET GO

In a perfect world . . .

Every author would have his or her entire manuscript—including all front matter, the main body, back matter—completed before he or she would submit it to PPG to begin the publication process.

In a perfect world, authors would also have scanned the shelves of the bookstores ahead of time to know exactly what types of book cover, interior designs, and fonts they would prefer to use for their books, and they would have all these instructions (along with their back cover copy) ready ahead of time to send along with their manuscript. This way, the back cover copy can be professionally copy edited along with the entire manuscript for consistency in style. Then authors would sit back and let the polishing process begin and watch their raw manuscripts take form as professional quality books. They would thoroughly enjoy the entire process and completely trust all the recommendations of the editors, designers, and proofreaders all along the way. Most importantly, they would trust themselves. They would trust that the book they have created is good enough as it is.

But this is far from a perfect world.

It never ceases to amaze me how many additional changes authors want to make to their books even after they've gone through the copy editing process. Copy editing is the very first step in the book publishing process. This step is where the majority of text changes (movements, additions, deletions, et cetera) are meant to take place. By the time the copy editing process is complete, the content itself should be complete for the most part. It should be where the author wants it.

Once the copy edit is complete, the raw edited manuscript and design instructions are given to the graphic designer to create the first draft of the actual book; and then a soft copy (.PDF) version of it goes back and forth between the designer and the author to tweak it here and there. For a very good reason, PPG only allows for two author-proofing rounds, including up to five structural changes to the cover and 50 typographical changes to the interior per round. (Additional charges apply to any additional proofing rounds ordered.) PPG makes this two-round rule because we know it is the nature of authors to pick and pick and pick at their own work—and we are saving them from themselves by limiting the amount of picking they can do. Otherwise, it would go on forever. That is the nature of the author—of *every* author, I've learned. (I assure you I totally understand. Not only am I a book publisher, but I'm also an author of five books that I picked at and picked at and picked at to the brink of insanity.)

As mentioned above, the purpose of this back and forth process between the author and graphic designer is to allow authors further opportunity to simply tweak (fine-tune) the content now that they can see it in actual book form. The time for major character changes and text block movements, additions, and deletions was long gone with the copy editing process; and now the purpose is simply to catch those last minute spelling errors and punctuation issues that were missed beforehand.

From there, once those two author-proofing rounds of the soft copy version of the book have been completed, a hard copy is ordered and sent to a professional proofreader for another once-over by yet another fresh set of eyes. If that proofreader notices anything else, those changes (which should be minimal by this stage) are completed and a final hard proof is sent to the author for final sign-off and approval.

It's an emotional process, this book publishing business. Authors' emotions and insecurities can get the best of them throughout this process, and it can make them second-guess their own decisions all along the way. At PPG, we understand this; and our book publishing process was developed and perfected with this in mind after extensive discussions and experience dealing with authors, copy editors, designers, proofreaders, indexers, you name it. If there's one piece of advice we want you to walk away with after reading this paragraph, it's this: it's good enough. Trust it. Trust yourself. (Of course, we're here to help. It's what we do best. You can trust that, too.)

WHEN TO WRITE? WHEN TO SELL? HOW TO GET IT ALL DONE?

Very recently, I received a note from an aspiring author who was overwhelmed by the sales and marketing aspect of book publishing and wanted to know when and how she is supposed to fit it all in. Here's my personal formula for writing, publishing, marketing, and selling my books. I'm not sure if it will work for you or not, but it's worth sharing with you nonetheless:

1. For each book I write, I set the goal: "I'd like the first draft completed by such-and-such a date." I always keep that promise to myself. I figure out how much time I need each month, week, and day to meet that goal date, and I discipline myself to do it.

2. After five books, my grown son now fully understands mom's process—and he knows to give me some space while I write so that I'm able to achieve these types of goals. (It is important to include family in your goals so they can help you achieve them. You may be surprised by just how supportive they are when you take the time to share your plans with them. They may even offer to help with some of the marketing.)

3. Once the first draft of my book is complete and with the copy editor, I switch from the writing gear into the sales and marketing gear. I begin blogging about the book and designing whatever other promo (e.g., "one sheets") that I will use to promote it; I begin contacting local book stores to set up near-future signings and readings; I think about what sort of video reading I might want to create to post on YouTube, and I start sending out invitations to the events via Facebook and email to generate interest ahead of time, et cetera.

4. Once the copy editor is done with his or her job in this process, I send the newly edited electronic version of the manuscript to my graphic designer along with my instructions, artwork, and author photo. While the designer sculpts all these raw materials into a professional-looking book, I'm still working full time, still being a mom, and still focused on my marketing plans. In fact, during several steps in this process, you'll be waiting for others to complete their various jobs (i.e., copy editing, graphic design, indexing, proofreading), so you might as well work on your sales and marketing at that time.

5. Once the book is officially published, now I'm "on tour" and working hard to promote it with Internet marketing, signings, and the like.

This is my process every time I publish a book. Although a book tour is meant to sell the most recent front list book, I always make sure to include promotional content for each previous back list book in the back matter of the new book (or, in the case of this book, within the body of it). I also bring the old books along to each event and sell them all as a series. (Every time I write a new book, I'm thinking, "How does this tie into the other books so I can sell them all as a series?") Do you see what I mean? Always thinking ahead.

On the PPG Publisher's Blog, you'll see a link to the Sales and Marketing category of the blog. There you will find all kinds of great ideas to help you sell your book. Everything you do has a cumulative effect. All these things work together over time, but make no mistake: there is NO substitute for in-person sales. It is the most effective way to move more books, and the author has to do it. Nobody can do it better for you.

HANDLING CRITICISM

When I published my first book, everything was quite new to me, and I had an expectation (possibly an unfair one) that my friends and family members should support me 100 percent and compliment me on my book no matter what they thought of it. Luckily, that did happen with my first book. Everyone around me was very supportive.

Unfortunately, when my second book came out, it was a different story. I received an unexpected criticism from someone dear to me that left me shocked, hurt, and unsure how to react. I'll be honest, it took me a couple years to come to a place where I was willing to put myself out there again. During that time, I had to rethink my expectations of those closest to me and find a way to remain confident in myself and in my craft regardless of others' opinions.

In retrospect, I'm glad I experienced that criticism so early in my publishing career because it taught me a valuable lesson about how I should measure the true merit of my work. A few times, I've had to ask myself the question: What is the truth here? Is it the joy and enthusiasm I felt when I held a printed copy of the book in my hand for the very first time? Or is it the self-doubt I felt when someone criticized it later on? Which one of those two moments will I use to determine the value of my book?

A wise woman named Lisa Nichols (2013) once said,

> Oftentimes, you give others the opportunity to create your happiness, and many times they fail to create it the way you want it. Why? Because only one person can be in charge of your joy ... and that's you. So even your parent, your child, your spouse—they do not have the control to create your happiness. They simply have the opportunity to share in your happiness. Your joy lies within you.

A beautiful sentiment, don't you think? I believe the same can be said for self-confidence and faith.

I've gone into every book project since then with a new set of expectations that take the pressure off both me and those around me. It's always nice when people acknowledge a new book with a hearty congratulations, but I've decided that's where their obligation ends. I no longer base a book's worth on whether others read it, agree with it, enjoy it, or discuss it with me after the fact. The truth I try my best to hold onto is the joy I felt when I held that first printed copy in my hand. I hope you will do the same for you. I hope you will find a way to hold onto your enthusiasm even if you come up against any criticism along the way—whether it's from friends, family members, reviewers, or anyone else. Keep writing! Keep the faith!

Author Mastermind Groups

You're not alone in this, you know. There are aspiring authors everywhere, and we can all benefit from each other's ideas and advice. That's the whole point of PPG's Author Mastermind Group on the PPG Writers Forum located at writersforum.polishedpublishinggroup.com.

A mastermind is a group of like-minded individuals with a common purpose and willingness to help each other solve problems. This group is where you can share your sales and marketing challenges and successes with other authors to help them out, while gleaning some inspiration of your own by learning about their experiences at the same time. Two heads are always better than one. Every PPG author deserves to be successful and, for all of us to be truly successful, we've got to help each other out.

Join the forum today and begin posting your comments and questions in the Author Mastermind Group. Someday, you'll be glad you did.

BIBLIOGRAPHY

Amazon. (2014a). *Kindle Direct Publishing Terms and Conditions.* Retrieved from https://kdp.amazon.com/help?topicId=APILE934L348N#Select

Amazon. (2014b). *Kindle Matchbook FAQ.* Retrieved from https://kdp.amazon.com/help?topicId=AVJCUBZXDNUM4

Amazon. (2014c). *Free Book Promotions FAQ.* Retrieved from https://kdp.amazon.com/help?topicId=A34IQoW14ZKXM9

Data ID Online. (2014). *What Is a Bar Code?* Retrieved from http://www.dataid.com/whatisbarcode.htm

ForeWord Reviews. (2014). *Clarion Reviews.* Retrieved from https://www.forewordreviews.com/services/book-reviews/clarion-review/

Free Dictionary, The. (2013). *Elevator Pitch.* Encyclopedia article about Elevator Pitch. Retrieved March 18, 2013, from http://encyclopedia.thefreedictionary.com/elevator+pitch

Eventbrite. (2013). *Join an Event Affiliate Program.* Eventbrite Help Centre. Retrieved March 18, 2013, from http://help.eventbrite.ca/customer/en_ca/portal/articles/426315

ISBN.org by Bowker. (2014). FAQs: *General Questions*. Retrieved from http://www.isbn.org/faqs_general_questions#isbn_faq1

Leschke, T. (2010). *The Index as a Roadmap*. Retrieved March 18, 2013, from PPG Publisher's Blog: http://blog.polishedpublishinggroup.com/2010/01/20/the-index-as-a-roadmap.aspx

Lynn, R. (2009, December 9). *Self-Publishers and Review Copies: Where and Why Self-Publishers Should Send Review Copies of Their Books*. Retrieved March 28, 2013, from PPG Publisher's Blog: http://blog.polishedpublishinggroup.com/2009/12/09/self-publishers-and-review-copies.aspx

Nichols, L. (2013). *The Secret by Rhonda Byrne*. Retrieved May 17, 2013, from Wattpad: http://www.wattpad.com/121164-the-secret-by-rhonda-byrne?p=35

Ortolon, J. (2013, March 15). *What's the point of using twitter?* Retrieved March 18, 2013, from Julie's Journal: http://www.juliesjournalonline.com/ whats-the-point-of-using-twitter/

Plank, R. (2013). *Sell Based on Value, Not Price*. Retrieved March 18, 2013, from Robertplank.com: http://www.robertplank.com/sell-based-on-value/

Polished Publishing Group. (2013a). *PPG Contests*. Retrieved March 18, 2013, from http://www.facebook.com/pages/Polished-Publish-ing-Group-PPG/245465516591#!/photo.php?fbid=10151151770376592&set=a.10150415163541592.353270.245465516591&type=1&theater

Polished Publishing Group. (2013b). *PPG Products & Services*. Retrieved March 18, 2013, from http://shop.polishedpublishinggroup.com/Book-Publishing-Services_c7.htm

Polished Publishing Group. (2013c). *PPG Publishing Agreement and Production Questionnaire*. Retrieved March 19, 2013, from http://www.polishedpublishinggroup.com/Publishing_Agreement_JHB6.html

Wikipedia. (2013a). *Digital Printing*. Retrieved March 28, 2013, from http://en.wikipedia.org/wiki/Digital_printing

Wikipedia. (2013b). *Elevator Pitch*. Retrieved March 18, 2013, from http://encyclopedia.thefreedictionary.com/elevator+pitch

Wikipedia. (2013c). *Offset Printing*. Retrieved March 28, 2013, from Wikipeida: http://en.wikipedia.org/wiki/Offset_printing

Wikipedia. (2013d). *Print on Demand*. Retrieved March 28, 2013, from http://en.wikipedia.org/wiki/Print_on_demand

Wikipedia. (2013e). *YouTube*. Retrieved March 18, 2013, from http://en.wikipedia.org/wiki/YouTube

INDEX

ABOUT THE AUTHOR

As a book publisher, Kim Staflund works with businesses and individuals around the world to produce superior quality ebooks, paperbacks, and hardcovers. As the founder and publisher at Polished Publishing Group (PPG), she has extensive experience with the traditional (trade), vanity, and supported self-publishing business models as both a service provider and an author. Kim built her company from the perspective of the author— taking the best practices from each business model to create a company that puts its authors first, while ensuring a professional, salable result.

Think of PPG as a skilled project manager for self-publishing authors. Using the supported self-publishing business model, the company assists authors in producing truly professional books by guiding them through the entire process from conception to publication. PPG helps both individuals and businesses to publish quality books and provides them with online distribution opportunities throughout the world.

In addition to her writing and book publishing background, Kim has a substantial sales and sales management history that includes new business development, both inside and outside account management of all types and sizes of companies, and personnel management and leadership experience within unionized and non-unionized environments. Add her firsthand knowledge of records management, process management, and project management into the mix and you have everything that is required in a professional book publisher to help authors everywhere succeed.

Kim's number one priority in each of these roles has always been, and will always be, to earn (and keep) the trust of each of her clients by providing honest, ethical, and thoughtful customer service that meets or exceeds their expectations.

BOOK REVIEWS

How to Publish a Book in Canada
. . . and Sell Enough Copies to Make a Profit!

eBook ISBN: 978-0-9864869-7-5 | Paperback ISBN: 978-0-9864869-6-8

"Staflund's stated goal is to give Canadian authors insight into what it takes to produce a salable book in Canada, get it into the hands of the desired demographic, and earn a healthy profit in the process. In this, she has succeeded admirably."

~ForeWord Reviews, Clarion Review

"A good source for writers of all experience levels seeking to publish quality books in Canada."

~Kirkus Reviews

"This book is a real, and I mean real, learning tool ... You will know how to do what the title states when you finish Kim Staflund's book."

~Palmetto Review

"*How to Publish a Book in Canada* is a very instructive book for any author—in and out of Canada. Though the book is specifically for Canadian authors, writers from any country will gain insight from this book."

~Pacific Book Review

"Staflund's personal stories, humor, and examples throughout makes this book entertaining as well as instructional . . . *How to Publish a Book in Canada* is a great investment for future publishers—both in Canada and outside of Canada."

~Penn Book Review

PolishedPublishingGroup
For Polished Professional Results

Main Website: www.polishedpublishinggroup.com

PPG Publisher's Blog: blog.polishedpublishinggroup.com

PPG Writers Forum: writersforum.polishedpublishinggroup.com

PPG Online Store: shop.polishedpublishinggroup.com

Facebook: www.facebook.com/pages/
Polished-Publishing-Group.../245465516591

Twitter: www.twitter.com/ppgpublishing

LinkedIn: www.linkedin.com/company/
polished-publishing-group-ppg-

Eventbrite: polishedpublishinggroup.eventbrite.ca

YouTube: www.youtube.com/user/PolishedPublishing

EzineArticles: EzineArticles.com/?expert=Kim_Staflund

Examiner: www.examiner.com/writing-in-calgary/kim-staflund